"Wars leave scars, as Tim Mallard knows all too well; he has himself been physically wounded in war and has also cared for hundreds of soldiers with invisible wounds. *In Moral and Spiritual Injury in War*, he helps us think about how to care for 'he [and she] who has borne the battle' and examines the ongoing, and lasting, damage done by the conflicts in Ukraine and the Middle East. Highly recommended for all who want to understand the most difficult of all human endeavors."

LTC (Retired) John Nagl, USA
Operation Desert Storm and
Operation Iraqi Freedom veteran
Author, *Learning to Eat Soup with a Knife*
and *Knife Fights: A Memoir of Modern War*

"Timothy Mallard—combat veteran, retired senior Army officer, military chaplain, scholar, educator, clergyman, ethicist—and survivor of moral injury brilliantly analyzes the nature of moral injury and spiritual injury, and why they matter to individuals and to societies. A 'must read.'"

General Vincent K. Brooks, U.S. Army (Retired)

"This ultimately hopeful book, by a man acquainted with grief, is a sobering reminder of the moral and spiritual costs of conflict. Written in the best traditions of pastoral theology, it converses with other disciplines while instilling confidence in the pastoral response. Crucially, the author goes beyond the personal needs of veterans to envisage a new dialogue between political, military, and religious leaders. His timely warning must be heeded—that moral and spiritual injury will deal with us unless we deal with it. In turn, that may keep us alert to the very values that are at stake in conflict."

Canon Andrew Totten OBE
Honorary Research Fellow
Durham University

"With prophetic insight and strategic clarity, Mallard elevates moral and spiritual injury from private struggle to national concern. Essential reading for leaders who steward both the soul of the warrior and the conscience of the profession."

Corie Weathers, LPC, BCC, NPC
Clinical Advisor on Military Morale & Leadership
Author, *Military Culture Shift*

"Timothy Mallard's book rests on the sure foundation of Christian just war thinking: first and foremost that the realm of war and insecurity is, like the rest of life, a realm of morality and responsibility. Moreover, his insights on the topics of moral injury and spiritual injury provide a valuable contribution for our guardians, chaplains, scholars, pastors, counselors, and concerned citizens."

Eric Patterson, PhD
President and CEO,
Victims of Communism Memorial Foundation

"This is a searching, compelling and, at times, highly personal exploration of Moral Injury from a vastly experienced US Army Chaplain. In also teasing out the nature of Spiritual Injury, and the strategic implications of these phenomena for contemporary and prospective conflicts, Dr. Mallard has added greatly to our understanding of both, and to their far-reaching effects in the military realm. In this, his first book, he has produced a fascinating and important text for pastors, service members, and policymakers alike."

Canon Professor Michael Snape FBA
Department of Theology and Religion,
Durham University

Timothy Mallard has given us a book that is at once deeply personal, profoundly learned, and urgently relevant. His decades as a U.S. Army Chaplain inform his approaches to spiritual and moral injury; they also shape his understanding of the nature of war. Most important of all, though, is how he braids together these threads. In Mallard's hands a strategic appraisal of moral injury emerges that illuminates how he views the kinds of care that future war requires.

Katherine Voyles, PhD, U.S. Army

"Physical injuries are often visible, drawing immediate compassion and aid. However, a deeper, more enduring, and unseen injury afflicts our warriors, units, and families—moral and spiritual injury. My hope is that leaders will confront this challenge directly and with courage. Chaplain (Colonel) Timothy Mallard, a devoted and compassionate leader of faith, will guide you through the fog, illuminating a path toward healing. This book deserves a place in every leader's kitbag."

CSM Robert Abernethy, U.S. Army (Ret.)

"Conflict is a constant in history but the application of violence in modern war is more complex than ever. The lack of clear ethics for combat in the space and cyber domains, as well as the proliferation of drones, robots, and other technology to replace humans in war, has increased the need for moral and spiritual guideposts on the battlefield. Dr. Timothy Mallard has charted a course for leaders to follow based on his nearly four decades of service in the U.S. Army. *Moral and Spiritual Injury in War* makes clear that moral and ethical awareness in warfare is more essential and challenging than ever. The growing entanglement of societies with combat forces, as demonstrated in Israel and Ukraine, clearly demonstrates the relevance of this book for all nations and audiences whose national security is under threat."

Major General John W. Weidner
U.S. Army

Timothy Mallard examines the immutable elements of conflict which characterize the nature of war amid the everchanging character of its prosecution—a future war which is more accurate, lethal, and which, ironically could be less discriminate, as population centers are increasingly targeted. The stakes could not be higher, as a paradigm characterized by maximalization rather than minimalization may be the outgrowth of autonomous weapon systems. What is the cost to the warrior, their families, and society and what is the prescription for mitigating these risks or ameliorating their effects? Utilizing modern case studies, Dr. Mallard illuminates the context and reveals that the underlying battlefield, individually, and nationally is spiritual. Remarkable work by this extraordinary warrior, chaplain, and healer of souls!

COL Kyle M. Walton, SF, U.S. Army (Ret.)
Former Commander, United States Military Observer Group

"Timothy Mallard captures moral and spiritual injury in refreshing and critical new ways. Herein, practitioners focused on helping others will find broadened and useful treatment methodologies; national security professionals will discover helpful decision-making and leader development frameworks; and those of us who reflect on our own combat experiences may finally discover the language necessary to express those experiences. I highly recommend Timothy's work to practitioners and academics alike."

Michael W. Rauhut, Combat veteran
Colonel, U.S. Army (Retired)

MORAL AND SPIRITUAL INJURY IN WAR

Russo-Ukraine, Israel-Iran, and Beyond

TIMOTHY S. MALLARD

STONE TOWER PRESS

Moral and Spiritual Injury in War: Russo-Ukraine, Israel-Iran, and Beyond

Stone Tower Press
7 Ellen Rd.
Middletown, RI 02842
stonetowerpress.com

Portions of Chapter 2 were originally published as "The (Twin) Wounds of War," in *Providence* (Winter 2016); 50–56 and are reprinted with permission..

All Scripture Citations are from the English Standard Version (ESV). Used with permission.

Paperback ISBN: 979-8-9919831-7-4

Formatting and cover design by Amy Cole, JPL Design Solutions

Printed in the United States of America

For Sharon, Thomas, Anna, and Caroline
and for
The Soldiers and Families it was my Honor to Serve

"There must, whether the gods see it or not,
be something great in the mortal soul.
For suffering, it seems, is infinite, and our capacity without limit."

C. S. Lewis

"And the man who really endured the War
at its worst was everlastingly differentiated
from everyone except his fellow soldiers."

Siegfried Sassoon

TABLE OF CONTENTS

LIST OF ABBREVIATIONS

ADO	All Domain Operations
AI	Artificial Intelligence
ASEAN	The Association of Southeast Asian Nations
AUKUS	Australia-United Kingdom-United States Trilateral Security Partnership
BRICS	Brazil-Russia-India-China-South Africa Intergovernmental Organization (also includes Iran, Egypt, Ethiopia, and the United Arab Emirates)
DIME-FIL	Diplomatic-Informational-Military-Economic-Financial-Intelligence-Law Enforcement (Instruments of National Power)
DOD	Department of Defense (United States)
DOS	Department of State (United States)
EU	The European Union
FPV	First Person View Drone
LAWS	Lethal Autonomous Weapons Systems
LSAWS	Lethal Semi-autonomous Weapons Systems
MI	Moral Injury
NATO	North Atlantic Treaty Organization
NSC	National Security Council
NDS	National Defense Strategy (United States)

NMS	National Military Strategy (United States)
NSS	National Security Strategy (United States)
PMIE	Potentially Morally Injurious Event
PTSD	Post-traumatic Stress Disorder
PTG	Post-traumatic Growth
SI	Spiritual Injury
UA	Unified Action
UAS	Uncrewed Aerial Systems
UGV	Uncrewed Ground Vehicles
USA	United States Army
USA	United States Air Force
USCG	United States Coast Guard
USFCC	United States Functional Combatant Commands (U.S. Cyber Command [CYBERCOM], U.S. Special Operations Command [SOCOM], U.S. Strategic Command [STRATCOM], and U.S. Transportation Command [TRANSCOM])
USGCC	United States Geographic Combatant Commands (U.S. Africa Command [AFRICOM], U.S. Central Command [CENTCOM], U.S. European Command [EUCOM], U.S. Indo-Pacific Command [INDOPACOM], U.S. Northern Command [NORTHCOM, and U.S. Southern Command [SOUTCOM])
USMC	United States Marine Corps
USN	United States Navy
USSF	United States Space Force

FOREWORD

I first met Chaplain Timothy Mallard just north of a decade ago at an annual meeting of the International Society of Military Ethics (ISME), then held at the University of Notre Dame. I was giving a breakout session paper on killing and the moral phenomenology of war that summarized elements from my soon-to-be-completed doctoral dissertation on just war and moral injury. I relied heavily on combat memoirs while also approaching the subject from a theological lens, drawing on Augustine, Thomas Aquinas, Nigel Biggar and other usual suspects. I was new to the ISME crowd and couldn't quite appreciate that my approach, while completely welcomed, was also somewhat rarely employed. As the session concluded, I was approached by a bear of an army lieutenant colonel whose build and bearing suggested rather an SF officer than the chaplain his uniform proved him to be. Nevertheless, the padre extended his hand with a warm smile and declared his delight that someone would invoke church fathers at a conference focused on martial themes. The ensuing conversation proved the bear was marbled with streaks of teddy bear. "Smitten" might not be quite the appropriate word, but we've been steadfast friends ever since.

It's no wonder really. My approach to military ethics is every bit Timothy's approach. Sometimes military chaplains are described—despairingly if not disparagingly—as having a "two-collar problem," symbolized by their wearing rank insignia on one uniform collar and chaplain insignia—in Timothy's case a cross—on the other. For some chaplains these different symbols mark a tension, even a contradiction. But the dual role of military officer and religious leader has never, to my knowledge, been a "problem" for Timothy. Rather, it was a boon and he leaned into it. His chaplaincy has been marked by theological strength fortified by worship in the broadest sense to include spiritual disciplines, religious practice, church history, theological reflection, prayer, biblical study, and right action. Timothy is also a student of war and he has mastered subjects germane to the vocation of arms: geopolitics, strategy, national security policymaking, organizational dynamics, leader development, the military and moral implications of new technologies, and stewardship of the profession. Together, these two great "texts" of faith and mission have fueled, not befuddled, Timothy's life of service to God, country, the warfighter, and those who support them.

A good foreword to a book usually must balance between highlighting the book's significance and contribution to its field of study and introducing, or establishing the credibility of, the author. My task is easier, for the book is the man behind it. By his own admission, Timothy, in this exemplary examination of moral and spiritual injury, owns the wounds of which he writes.

The spiritual and moral demands made of warfighters were made clear to Timothy while stationed at the Department of Defense headquarters, the Pentagon, on September 11, 2001. That morning, he happened to be several miles away at home taking care of a sick child when, despite the distance, he heard American Airlines Flight 77 collide into the Pentagon's west side. In the best tradition of the American warrior, Timothy, knowing what was needed, immediately rushed toward the danger. Over the next days he served wherever necessary: helping to rescue, shore up building sections, recovering the dead, supporting victims and their families, and ministering.

One morning, as Timothy arrived at the chaplain's tent, an exhausted FEMA team told him they weren't going back into the building until he spoke to them and gave them some message of hope. Grief and trauma and the sheer helpless magnitude of their task was overwhelming them, and morale was low. Timothy turned to Psalm 23 and began to read, "Yea, though I walk through the valley of the shadow of death …" He then paused and looked over to the terrible wound the attack had torn in the side of the Pentagon and began crying. The tears were a blessing. "Maybe that gave others permission to start crying as well," Timothy reflected. He then realized he had to finish the rest of the Psalm. When he had done so, one of the FEMA workers said, "Okay, now we're ready to go." And they did.

Military chaplains are rightly called "force multipliers" because they punch above their weight, enhancing the effectiveness of military units beyond their direct role as spiritual and pastoral caregivers. At their best, Chaplains bolster the resilience and moral vigor—and therefore the lethality—of warfighters by attending to their spiritual well-being in numerous ways: offering ethical guidance, crisis intervention, family care, and trusted counsel. But this service can come at personal costs.

After the FEMA team left to get on with their mission, Timothy returned to the chaplain tent, found a dark corner, and wept. In the Jewish tradition, the *Tzadik* (צדיק) is a highly righteous person, often a spiritual leader or master, who is considered a bridge between humanity and God. They are admired for their piety, their basic decency, and their ability to guide others. But they also are admired for bringing into themselves the hurts and harms and horrors of the world. By making these sorrows their own, the *Tzadikim* lighten the burdens of others and allow them to get on with what needs to be done. The world could not function without the likes of such as these.

It may be, though I think not, too much to suggest that Timothy is a *Tzadik*, but—and while sticking to the tradition but switching languages—Timothy is for certain a remarkable *mensch*. Trafficking as he does in matters of human mortality, killing, sin, and tragedy, Timothy may well own the wounds of which he writes, but he also owns the integrity, courage, faith, patriotism, heroism, honor, and deep love of neighbor of which he writes as well.

Timothy is a warrior who has served at the tactical, operational, and strategic levels of conflict but who has never forgotten that he is also a shepherd. This mustn't be misunderstood. As shepherd, Timothy may have a flock, but that flock is a pack and his sheep are wolves. For nearly forty years, Timothy has pastored men and women of tremendous individual and collective kinetic force. He has not shied away from readying them for the fight. But he is conscious that even fighting right fights rightly can be perilous. Timothy is fond of quoting Karl Marlantes, who is in his wonderful *What It Is Like to Go to War* writes, "the violence of combat assaults psyches, confuses ethics, and tests souls. This is not only a result of the violence suffered. It is also a result of the violence inflicted." Because of this, and like another of his heroes who he quotes in this book, Timothy knows that his primary task is shepherding the souls of his warriors.

All this is now deeply personal. As I write, my son is carefully choosing between offers of admission into the Corps of Cadets at Texas A&M and the US Military Academy at West Point. Whichever pathway he chooses, in four years' time, it is my prayer that he will commission into an army is still marked by the warrior care that Timothy Mallard has given it so well and for so long. Timothy—and General Marshall—are right: the soldier's soul is everything. This book, drawn from Timothy's long decades of dedicated service to our nation's warfighters, is a study in soul care. As a grateful father I am heartily glad he has written it.

Marc LiVecche
McDonald Distinguished Scholar
of Ethics, War, and Public Life;
and adjunct professor of ethics,
US Naval Academy.
Author of *The Good Kill: Just War and Moral Injury*

PREFACE

At the risk of being overly confessional, I admit that I have always questioned why an author writes a book. As a reader, I have found it compelling to know what motivates that author to engage in such an unforgiving and daunting task. Thus, in fidelity to you, the reader, allow me to detail why I chose now to put pen to paper on the topic of moral and spiritual injury in war.

Firstly, I have served in the profession of arms for over three decades, all in uniformed service as an active-duty U.S. Army chaplain. More than this, my father was also an active-duty U.S. Army chaplain for over three decades. While his experience was neither paradigmatic nor prescriptive for me, still, I have spent much of my life as a child, teen, young adult and adult in this unique context and it deeply informs me, both personally and professionally. Indeed, I first came face to face with deep-seated moral injury and spiritual injury through my father, who served as a battalion chaplain with the 1st Cavalry Division in Vietnam and lived these internal injuries as his woundedness became our woundedness as a family. Now at the conclusion of my own military career, leaving such a consuming familial and professional ethos is the next calling in my life, a project which I confess fills me with not a little anxiety, questioning, and desire for clarity.

Secondly, as mentioned, I served in the U.S. Army for almost thirty-seven years. As a noncombatant Army chaplain, I have never seen a more pastorally complex and contested ministry environment in which to serve. The issues of human mortality, killing, redemption, service to God and the state, familial transition and stress, pain and woundedness, the burden of leadership, directing complex organizations, the pace and rapidity of new technologies, the increasingly fraught threat environment—all of these and more drive the ethically and morally ambiguous context of soldiering each day, both in peace and war. In one sense, I admit that this context has often shaped me in very inchoate ways, where only later did I realize that where I thought I was often acting independently of any other influences, I was far more influenced by the military culture around me than I knew. Nonetheless, mine has hopefully been a journey of continued self-awareness and growth in understanding, nowhere more than as I moved from serving at the tactical to the operational and then the strategic levels of war. When finally illuminated, I have tried to gently shape the culture around me, only to feel inadequate in doing so, or that the vital moment had passed by me.

Thirdly, as a component of my development, I have never lost a continued desire to theologically question, study, and grow relative to the weightiest professional issues of this military calling. Continued reading, biblical study, and theological reflection and writing have been important touchstones of my desire to minister to units and commands in which I've served. In this vein, however, I am very concerned. Indeed, I believe that with the general diminution of religious influence in the American public square, there has been a concomitant erosion within the profession of arms to allow religious concepts, truths, and admonitions to be heard with force—particularly within the ranks. Although I am in no way advocating for theology to become prescriptive for the profession of arms, I am concerned that theology's influence has waned to the point that warriors risk forgetting—and thus employing—enduring religious and moral values, principles, beliefs, and ethical leadership lessons which previous generations found paradigmatic to a healthful service to both God and country. Thus here, in studying moral and spiritual injury in war, I am decidedly placing myself squarely in the discipline of pastoral theology. I do this to not only remain in keeping with my service as a chaplain but also to add a distinctly different voice than that of the clinical or martial disciplines which so often dominate the contemporary discussion on these topics.

This said, I have been greatly informed by the non-theological questioning, study, and growth which has marked my career across these years. Never whilst I was in seminary or divinity school did I consider that I would one day study—let alone teach—lessons on theological topics like moral and spiritual injury in war as well as on non-theological topics like geopolitics, national security policymaking, organizational dynamics, leader development, stewarding the profession, or the defense industrial base as do I today. Nonetheless, reading, reflection, and writing on these and other topics have been important milestones in my continued growth as a military leader.

Nowhere is this more critical than relative to the specialty of ethics in the profession of arms. The voices of many theological ethicists, to be sure, have been critical but so have those of moral philosophers, secular ethicists, political theorists, and, of course, warriors within the profession. Attending to many other streams of learning has been a part of the rich process of development which has brought me to this book. This includes in no small measure my residency within that politico-philosophical community of Christian Realism (so-called) and ethical community of the Just War Tradition, both camps into which I consciously stand.[1] I contend that both these perspectives are vitally necessary to the present and future continuation of the healthful democratic project in America and, more specifically, the profession of arms of this nation. I recognize that others would disagree with my positions, but I hold them consciously and vigorously.

For these reasons the reader deserves to at least know these prejudices about me as the author of this work. While aware of my biases and attempting to reflect and write objectively as I possibly can, I cannot completely uncouple myself from these influences. Theologically, God would certainly not have me do so, for anything which shapes me is in fact a part of His calling upon my life. Notwithstanding this, however, I take this tack consciously and with appreciation and openness to the critique of other perspectives, whether from differing faith traditions, nationalities, political philosophies, or moral and ethical stances, etc.

Within the uniquely American context of civil-military relations, there is an additional caveat. One of the military roles of a chaplain is, doctrinally, to serve as "the conscience of the command."[2] This role embodies one of my professional motivations for what is to follow in this work, evocatively (and not provocatively) describing a problem within the ranks I inhabit. Nevertheless, I was a serving, commissioned officer of the republic and remain governed by the American civil-military construct, of which a basic premise is that such officers do not make political critiques or decisions. That indeed is not my intent in this work. However, the contemporary profession of arms is much more complex than this historical principle might initially indicate.

Today, there is a considered call for serving, commissioned officers as myself to be more attuned to the political nature of the contemporary profession of arms, for the military instrument of power is increasingly and inextricably linked to the political instrument of power for the United States, or any nation.[3] While upholding an officer's subservience to civilian political authority, in such a context, I do seek to reflect and write on the pressing nature of moral and spiritual injury and how these outgrowths of war are rapidly becoming pressing ethical concerns relative to future war.

Additionally, I believe that the Just War Tradition—including the growing usage of its component stages of *jus ante bellum* (right preparation before war), *jus ad bellum* (right decision-making to initiate war), *jus in bello* (right conduct of war), and *jus post bellum* (right restoration after war)—has a tremendous role to play in helping nations to strategically think about moral and spiritual injury, both for their military forces and for their civilian citizens. This further bespeaks that this topic is one of first importance not only for American but also for professional militaries of other nations with whom we will conduct future unified actions. Moral and spiritual injury are strategic problems of future war for every modern military force and nation, and we either attend to them now or they will attend to us later. Describe it as sounding a tocsin, perhaps, but in the vein of being a "loving, loyal, connected critic," it is time to draw attention to this phenomenon and its strategic implications.[4]

Some thanks are in order. As with all works, my thoughts are my own and thus all mistakes are my own, in whole or in part. I look forward to and welcome all who will provide critique and dialogue over the issues which I raise here in this work. As well, I need to offer thanks to many who have supported me in this endeavor. First, I am indebted to Tim Demy and the team at Stone Tower Press, without whose belief in me, sharp dialogue, and patient encouragement, you the reader would not hold this book in your hands. Second, this work largely arose from an elective course I developed and taught for three years at the United States Army War College, so I am in debt to the college for the opportunity to candidly broach a difficult subject with the profession of arms. Moreover, it was the passion, experience, pain, and insights of my students that sharpened my own thinking on these topics and motivated me to write this book. This is in no small way a debt I owe to them and their families, and I learned far more from them than I ever taught. Third, I must publicly recognize Dr. Thomas DeGraba, Dr. Peter Brooks, and the entire team of healers at the National Intrepid Center of Excellence at Walter Reed National Military Medical Center in Bethesda, MD. Without this team of caring healers, I would never have left the wilderness of injury which plagued my life for so many years. Fourth, I am grateful to the warm, supportive faculty of St. Chad's College at Durham University and of the Department of Theology and Religion—particularly Principal Margaret Masson, Professor Simon Oliver, and Professor Michael Snape—who afforded me time, resources, and encouragement to finish this work during our year-long sabbatical after retiring from the U.S. Army. Fifth, I owe thanks to my colleagues at the International Centre for Moral Injury, especially Dr. Brian Powers and Dr. Jane Lidstone, whose friendship and mutual interest were of immense value in completing this work. Sixth, I must laud my colleagues at the journal *Providence* and at the Institute on Religion and Democracy—especially Dr. Marc LiVecche, Mr. Mark Tooley,

Dr. Eric Patterson, and Dr. Dan Strand—who were friends more than anything, but who have continually supported me and my work.

Finally, I must thank my wife Sharon and our children Thomas, Anna, and Caroline, who will no doubt see themselves and us in these pages, but who nonetheless walked this road without being asked and who became the vessels of my and our recovery. I love you all more than I can say, and only pray that you can see—despite our woundedness—that God is leading us towards a brighter and living hope.

Timothy Mallard
St. Chad's College, Durham University, United Kingdom
Ash Wednesday 2025

1

BOUNDARY CROSSING: MORAL INJURY

The Strategic Context and Problem

This book explores the intersection between current war, moral and spiritual injury in warriors and families, ethics in the profession of arms, strategic national security, and future war. In a way that will be detaiedl below, there is an unexamined relationship between these seemingly disparate topics. This book, however, does not solely explore moral injury, particularly individual concerns about its descriptive markers, treatment modalities, clinical history and academic currents, or even theological and pastoral responses. Many others have expertly and ably explored all these as discrete topics relating to moral injury. As stated, however, this book is a different tack. Why so?

In my estimation, war as a collective human phenomenon is reemerging as an ever-present, multivalent problem, not easily constricted to historical examples and fast morphing into new global problem sets. Indeed, war is now a major daily concern—if not a direct experience—for millions of people. For instance, it would be reductionist to confine our understanding of contemporary war either through the prism of the geopolitically catastrophic American exit from Afghanistan or from several decades of other intrastate or substate global counterinsurgency conflicts such as in Iraq, Libya, or the Sahel.

Comparatively, the global impact of new state-level conflicts resulting from Russia's 2022 invasion of Ukraine and Hamas's 2023 attack into Israel (and it's resulting conflicts in Lebanon, Syria, and Iran, as well as the related Iranian proxy war in the Red Sea), ongoing historical flashpoints such as in either Taiwan or the China-India or India-Pakistan borders, and regional tensions such as between Iran and Saudi Arabia or Colombia and Venezuela—all have reminded us that state on state and great power tensions and conflicts are alive and well.[1] Indeed, as one recent U.S. government bipartisan report stated in assessing the 2022 National Defense Strategy (NDS) prioritization of threats:

> The strategic environment in summer 2024 presents more, and vastly more serious, challenges to U.S. security interests than the since the end of the Cold War, if not the height of World War II. Many of the threats are intertwined and compounding, making them more difficult to overcome... we believe that the magnitude of the threats the United States faces is understated and significantly worse than when the NDS was issued, especially when viewed globally and as compounding. Since the release of the NDS, we have witnessed but not fully accounted for the strategic impact of the "no limits" partnership between Russia and China and their partnership with Iran and North Korea, the outbreak of war in the Middle East, and the scope and duration of war in Europe.[2]

Additionally, the character of war is changing, whilst the nature of war is remaining remarkably resilient.[3]

As the profession of arms has moved decisively into the era of all-domain operations (so war simultaneously and continuously in and through land, sea, air, space and cyberspace) and is framed as an ever-present state of geopolitical competition (rather than any hope for a return to a post-conflict state of a just, "rightly ordered" peace), conflict seems now to be a never-ceasing quality of the human condition.[4] We have warrant to question whether Augustine's ideal remains strategically valued: "Peace between a mortal man and his Maker consists in ordered obedience, guided by faith, under God's eternal law; peace between man and man consists in regulated fellowship… .Peace, in its final sense, is the calm that comes of order (*pax omnium rerum tranquillitas ordinis*)."[5]

This notwithstanding, historical strategic challenges in war remain. Among these are things such as the proliferation and use of new technology (for example, as with artificial intelligence (AI) or semi-autonomous and autonomous lethal weapons systems—S-LAWS and LAWS). There is also the latent threat of nuclear weapons, the emergence of new chemical or biological weapons. One might further add the increasingly problematic concerns around transnational refugee movements, resource constraints and disputes, and ensuring ongoing access to sea, air and space routes. In sum, war is clearly now a "wicked problem," and observers of the scene must remain adept in adapting our expectations about war to its changing character and context while being sanguine about its historic challenges to human and societal flourishing.[6]

Into this decisively changed strategic context, a latent but growing problem has arisen: the phenomenon of moral injury. First conceptually developed in America in the mid-1990s relative to clinical therapeutic work with Vietnam veterans, the basic concept has now exploded in both understanding and application, perhaps to the point of confusion and confusion. Today, it has gained increasingly nuanced understandings across broad facets of the psychiatric, psychological, medical, pastoral, martial, ethical, and theological disciplines, to name but a few. Indeed, today moral injury is increasingly (and welcomingly) being applied to traumas of personal internal woundedness in fields of study and work such as with survivors of sexual assault, veterinarian care of animals, non-governmental assistance to refugees and displaced persons, and even violations of ethical standards in corporate business.

Notwithstanding this trend noted above, this work will remain focused on the singular context of the profession of arms but will expand its application from not only the tactical level but also the operational and strategic levels of war.[7] Indeed, a fresh and expanded strategic appraisal of moral injury is now required. This woundedness is now an unexamined but critical outcome of contemporary war. Indeed, in this book, I pair moral and spiritual injury together, as I see them as "twin children" of the same martial parent of war. However, far from simply being only a tactical problem to consider anymore in terms of a singular focus on diagnosis, treatment modalities, etc., moral and spiritual injury are strategic problems of future war for every modern military force and nation, and we either address them now or they will imperil us later.

What are moral and spiritual injury? We'll attend to this critical question shortly, but prior to doing so, we must examine some of my biases on these topics, because they clearly attenuate how I will view the problem and its solutions. First and as previously mentioned, my status as a retired U.S. Army chaplain informs my perspectives on all that will be written about below. I cannot undo my collective experiences of over three decades of active-duty pastoral service, either in peace or in war, and certainly sometimes whether I would want to do so or not. Some memories from these experiences are so prevalent that they have marred my mind and soul, and any reader deserves to know this at the outset.

I have been diagnosed with both Post-traumatic Stress Disorder and mild Traumatic Brain Injury, interior wounds of my mind not easily visible to others, but whose outward effects can and have been clinically diagnosed and treated by experts. At times, this has left me feeling as if I am a "Shepherd of Ghosts," because these memories live *with* me wherever I go: they disturb my sleep; they make me hyper vigilant to external stimuli; they prompt me to escape crowds; they spark angry outbursts even to those whom I love the most; they at times weigh me down with grief and sorrow; and they sometimes prevent me from feeling the pain of others, even when I should. That said, I have been expertly treated and supported by a great cadre of clinical and spiritual healers across many years, who have often helped me see myself in new ways and have provided, perhaps most importantly, a restoration of self-understanding about my context. Without them, I would not be here, and all I can do is render them thanks and admiration for their mastery of applying the caring arts to me and to my family.[8] While I cannot and would not disown this facet of my life, every reader deserves to know this about the hand behind these words. I own the wounds of which I write.

A second facet of my experience as an Army "Padre" is that this continues to shape how I conceptually think about, apply language to, and propose solutions for the problems of moral and spiritual injury. Indeed, mine has been a pastoral and theological calling to serve in the profession of arms and I am, as the late Larry Kent Graham termed it, "a physician of fractured souls."[9] This is decidedly different from any clinical or therapeutic professionals living out a calling to that same profession, which would seem almost self-evident. Why, then, is this important?

Firstly, I have unfortunately all too often seen fellow chaplains who—for a variety of reasons—have ventured out of their pastoral and theological identities and attempted to take on either a proto-clinical or proto-therapeutic identity in then serving warriors and families. Indeed, some of my chaplain colleagues have pursued education, supervision, and licensure to attain therapeutic standing, but sometimes at the cost of their pastoral calling. I have immense respect for and have been expertly treated by many clinical and therapeutic professionals—but I am not one of their ranks. Similarly, they are not one of my ranks. That said, we are allies in the great wholistic cause of treating warriors and families body, mind, and spirit, but I maintain that the spirit here is not an appendage, it is core to a person's being.[10]

This leads, secondly, however, to a decided trend in the profession of arms (as across many particularly western societies), and that is to afford both the clinical and therapeutic professions an outsized importance in terms of comprehensively diagnosing and treating warriors and families who are injured in any way, shape, or form. Indeed, as Simon Edwards noted:

> The neglect of the spiritual dimension in treating mental health can largely be ascribed to the secularization of the culture in which the mainly science-based clinical disciplines have developed. Yet this contrasts with the culture of the military that is unique in the public sector as recognizing the importance of the spiritual side of the human condition... The military is exclusive in public services in understanding the importance of the soul. Chaplains still deploy on operations. Yet when it comes to dealing with the consequences of combat, this element is almost totally neglected.[11]

There will be more to say on this later, but for now, it is enough to note that I do not subscribe to the assumption that any comprehensive recovery from all internal woundedness in warriors and families is only and always a function of solely a clinician or a therapist; frankly, and in my experience, wise clinicians and therapists also admit this truth. Indeed, our very contemporary understanding of moral and spiritual injury was borne out of the frustrations of clinicians and therapists who felt they were observing a type of internal woundedness that their professional acumen could not readily name or describe. A "Padre," however, is comfortable in this space, because this type of injury is an outgrowth of the soul. This informs how and what is offered here.

With this as a given, then, what are the possible assumptions about how to best approach this topic? Put another way, what "lenses" might I admit that I wear in viewing the problems of moral and spiritual injury? Beyond my professional experience detailed above, I see, at a minimum, three such assumptions relative to our topic: one's experiences of either combat or trauma; one's experience in treating others dealing with their experiences of either combat or trauma; and, or, one's employment of applied ethics in the profession of arms.[12] These "lenses" become powerful frameworks that connote a person's underlying values, attitudes, beliefs, and assumptions, and which—if left unexamined—can quickly overwhelm any dispassionate examination of a subject or ability to dispositively comment on a fresh way ahead from any problem set. In essence, this is a critically important issue, for how one thinks about war—and its attendant problems such as moral and spiritual injury—must rise to the level of self-awareness, else one's unexamined values, principles, and beliefs will quickly become immovable biases, heuristics, and prejudices.

If one of these three lenses, then, is possibly operative for each of us as we examine the topic of moral and spiritual in war, how best should we surface them to a level of self-awareness? A helpful method here may perhaps be to articulate the questions that undergird our interest, or even which linger just below even that level of cognition. For instance, as an American, as a member of the profession of arms, as an Army chaplain and military ethicist, and as a fellow sufferer, here I see five possible questions that I have heard voiced by warriors and family members in approaching this issue:

- How do I make sense of my raw, internal woundedness brought on by war?
- Can I trust my government with its stated national aims in war?
- Can I recover my morale (and lead others) for future service in the profession of arms?
- Have I (and/or my family) reached a moral and ethical inflexion point in my vocation of uniformed service, such that continued service is an open question?
- How can I, if possible, healthfully live with this for the rest of my life?[13]

My purpose here in listing these questions is not to answer them, for that is an individual project for each person. Rather, I simply wish to raise them to a level of awareness at the outset of this book, because these have become the internal questions which I have heard warriors and families increasingly wrestle with in the past 20 or so years.

If these are their "lenses"—and perhaps one or more resonates with any reader of this book—then without answering them here, we must be comfortable to be aware of them and hold them aside in tension while we reflect on moral and spiritual injury in war. However, what we can see from them is the complex interplay of internal woundedness, individual identity, meaning, and purpose, extension of that woundedness to those in closest relationship around us, and even extension of that woundedness to the profession of arms and our wider culture and body politic. Essentially, neither moral nor spiritual injury occurs in a vacuum; rather, they have concentric impact on an ever-expanding circle of relationships. We need to recover this linkage between internal woundedness and relationship, because ironically, it was always at the heart of the initial effort to name and describe this malady.

Moral Injury in War Today—Two Questions

So, now we are prepared to delve more closely into first understanding moral injury. To start, there are two questions that seem to naturally lend themselves to our inquiry:

1. What is the definition of moral injury?
2. Where is one wounded through moral injury?

Although these questions may seem easy enough to voice, they are frustratingly complex to answer.

As to a definition, there are two models which dominate the discourse. In the American context, clinicians helping Vietnam veterans after the close of that conflict began discerning a trend in combat survivors which gradually came to be termed moral injury. Psychologist Jonathan Shay first explored the moral meaning of combat and military service, particularly relative to the United States war in Vietnam, in his classic book *Achilles in Vietnam* and then in his social exploration of that war on the nation in his follow-on *Odysseus in America*.[14]

Shay saw in the troubled moral reflectivity of his patients many parallels to Homer's *Iliad* and other characters from Greek tragedy and philosophy. Essentially, Shay was arguing that moral injury was neither a new phenomenon nor one that could be segregated only to those warriors it troubled. Rather, this was an intractable type of injury that, as with the ancient Greeks, affected all of society.[15]

Arising from these works, Shay then defined the term moral injury in a groundbreaking article in 2014. Again, and relative only to the profession of arms, he opined: "Moral injury is:

- A betrayal of what's right.
- By someone who holds legitimate authority (e.g., in the military—a leader).
- In a high stakes situation."[16]

Now again, Shay coined the term from noting the prevalence of problems of moral decision-making in these veterans who were his therapeutic clients. Indeed, Shay he saw in them a pattern in their internal woundedness which seemed to stand outside the clinical criteria for PTSD, which again, is an observable disorder of the mind that is manifested in both interior changed thought processes as well as outward behaviors.[17]

Moreover, Shay saw in his veterans clients—particularly those who had experienced prolonged, close and intense combat—a trend which manifested itself in intense emotional feelings and deep, reflective self-questioning.[18] This led to his further observation that combat significantly degrades how warriors understand their own moral frameworks and degrades their ability to evaluate right and wrong choices and thus how such choices need to be appropriately decided in future under stressful circumstances.[19]

Why was this type of injury so deleterious? One of the critical—and often under presented—observations which Shay made was his immediate emphasis on the social effects of moral injury. Again, drawing from Greek mythology, Shay correlates it to the Greek term *themis*, which he connotes as encompassing moral order, convention, normative expectations, ethics, and commonly understood social values. Moreover, this communal norm of *themis* then becomes paradigmatic for a military force, which becomes a its own moral entity. He states:

> Any army, ancient or modern, is a social construction defined by shared expectations and values. Some of these are embodied in formal regulations, defined authority, written orders, ranks, incentives, punishments, and formal task and occupational definitions. Others circulate as traditions, archetypal stories of things to be emulated or shunned, and accepted truth about what is praiseworthy and what is culpable. All together, these form a moral world that most of the participants most of the time regard as legitimate, "natural," and personally binding. The moral power of an army is so great that it can motivate men to get up out of a trench and step into enemy machine-gun fire.[20]

To return to defining moral injury, however, clinician Ed Tick built on the communal emphasis of Shay and aided in exploring the social isolation in which Vietnam veterans deployed to, fought in and redeployed from war, and how, in the American context, society reinforced their isolation from the *polis*.

Tick noted that Vietnam produced the sending and receiving of warriors in a vacuum without any social connection to the fight to which the nation asked them to go, a particular loss being of any religious blessing or restoration practices that accompanied past conflicts.[21] Derivatively, Larry Dewey helpfully delineated the power of collective sharing of story in effecting healing in Vietnam Veterans, noting that for many who had experienced severe PTSD, the supportive nurture of fellow warriors in a group setting allowed them to re-explore traumatic experiences which they had buried in silence for decades.[22]

Finally, my late colleague, Chaplain (Colonel) Herman "Herm" Keizer, U.S. Army, was instrumental in establishing the Soul Repair Center at Brite Divinity School at Texas Christian University. Though the center remains there, it has now spawned the Shay Center for Moral Injury, that operates under the aegis of the Volunteers of America and that remains a leader for the public awareness and treatment of moral injury in severely traumatized warriors.[23]

Collectively, these and other thinkers, clinicians, chaplains, and pastors have helped map what moral injury looks like in warriors. This includes markers such as: a pervasive guilt leading to unforgiveness; the "shrinkage" of one's moral horizon; the development of prevailing hopelessness; a social distance from community and creation; and a diminished future capacity to distinguish right from wrong (or to exercise a morally nuanced reflectivity).[24]

Indeed, it is from precisely trying to respond to the care needs for warriors and families (particularly in terms of the rising suicide attempt and completion rates for actively serving warriors and then post-service veterans) that the second dominant definition of moral injury arose. The now standard definition of moral injury has come from experts in the field at the U.S. Department of Veterans of Affairs (though the explanation of the phenomenon is more descriptive than proscriptive).[25] The VA definition has now become an oft-cited reference in the clinical study and treatment of moral injury and states:

> Like psychological trauma, moral injury is a construct that describes extreme and unprecedented life experience including the harmful aftermath of exposure to such events (e.g. combat trauma). Events are considered morally injurious if they "transgress deeply held moral beliefs and expectations." Thus, the key precondition for moral injury is an act of

> transgression, which shatters moral and ethical expectations that are rooted in religious or spiritual beliefs, or culture-based, organizational, and group-based rules about fairness, the value of life, and so forth.[26]

Although this definition is a helpful advance, my concern with it is three-fold.[27] First, is the distinct contrast with Shay's noun of betrayal, as this definition shifts to a less provocative, yet manifestly theological concept of transgression —which particularly in Christian theology is tied to the antecedent concept of "sin" and the descendent concept of "forgiveness"—without any linkage between the three concepts. To be fair, of course, neither Litz, Maguen, or any of the others who helped craft this definition are theologians, and they should not be expected to be such. However, perhaps that illumines the problem. With linguistic and cultural ties to an orison so paradigmatic as The Lord's Prayer, something that millions of people with even minimal Christian faith often recite weekly and with an emphasis on "forgive us our trespasses as we forgive those who trespass against us…" (Matthew 6:12), the noun "transgression" can seem discordant, as it is built on a theological understanding but with no integration of its theological roots or resolution.

Secondly and again in contrast to Shay, this definition grammatically lacks a subject. Utilizing the passive voice, the subject is opaque (perhaps intentionally so), and so the perpetrator of the moral injury may be either the warrior herself or someone opposed to the warrior who has done something against her. While the flexibility is perhaps academically or clinically preferred, I am concerned as an ethicist that it also hides the issue of moral agency which is critical to discerning cause and effect. The warrior could be presumed to have somehow "transgressed" a moral code; conversely, another could be presumed to have "transgressed" a moral code against the warrior. Because this is a work concerned with theological ethics, then, this distinction is critical, because ethics as a discipline is concerned with linking cause and effect, or more accurately at least attending to agency and action.[28] By this definition, the subject is left unidentified, and the moral agency and responsibility of that person is thus unassignable. Again, while a moral boundary is crossed, the definition clouds moral accountability, but candidly, war is almost never so opaque. People act or fail to act, and this results or fails to result in the intended effect, an ambiguous environment in which warriors long more than anything for clarity, and understanding.

Thirdly, the definition appears to locate moral injury and its spiritual and even religious component under the broader framework of moral philosophy rather than moral theology, but I think that this is in fact the wrong way around. Stated alternatively, religious belief and spiritual praxis have historically been seen as the construct under which morality resides rather than the converse, though this point is certainly contested in contemporary secular philosophies.

Recall that the accepted clinical definition neatly packages transgression of a religious code or belief system under morality writ large. But, is there a major religious belief system in the world in which human morality is presumed to be the progenitor of belief rather than the opposite? Indeed, most religious systems hold that humans are presumed to be (if active in their religious confession) bearers of that belief in their thoughts, words, and deeds.[29] This is Augustinian in nature in that doing is presupposed to arise from our being (and thus God has changed our being through belief and reshaped our lived actions).[30] Relative to the injuries warriors experience in combat, then, we cannot segregate any discussion of how religious belief and practice can influence our understanding of to treat such injured warriors, and moreover we must properly balance our understanding of moral injury under a larger construct of both clinical insight and religious belief in general.[31] Notwithstanding these points, however, the above definition of moral injury is a helpful descriptor, at the least as a starting point for our collective understanding and reflection.

More recently, I have been pleased to join in the efforts of the International Centre for Moral Injury (ICMI), located at Durham University, England, a dedicated scholarly consortium that has made admirable contributions to the broadening understanding and application of moral injury both within and without the military contexts that first bounded Jonathan Shay's work. The ICMI's collective definition of moral injury now builds on both Shay and VA definitions to this nuanced articulation:

> Moral Injury refers to the experience of sustained and enduring negative moral emotions—guilt, shame, contempt and anger—that results from the betrayal, violation or suppression of deeply held or shared moral values. It is distinct from post-traumatic stress disorder (PTSD), which entails the body and mind's adaptation to situations of extreme fear and stress. Moral Injury involves a profound sense of broken trust in ourselves, our leaders, governments and institutions to act in just and morally "good" ways.[32]

This definition helpfully captures several salient points. First, it incorporates Shay's original verb of betrayal to capture the extent to which someone can feel moral injury, almost in a visceral way. This recaptures Shay's implied emphasis on relationships as being the critical context for moral injury. Further, by qualifying it as both "sustained and enduring," it further links moral injury to the qualifier of time, which is a critical factor in our understanding of why this injury is so debilitating—it is both "pervasive and persistent" to the core of one's being and to the whole of one's life.[33]

Second, it leaves space for the possibility that moral injury can be something that is done to one from outside the self through a "violation or suppression" of deeply held or even shared moral values, notwithstanding that moral silence and inaction in the face of ethical decision-making can be, by an individual, a type of self-violation or suppression of those same values. Here, the ICMI definition better alludes to the concept of moral agency, and thus cause and effect.

Third, the definition helps addresses a common question on the part of many: how is moral injury different from PTSD? However, it only glosses on this difference, and as we will see below, a full understanding of both concepts must be employed to effectively distinguish between the two concepts.

Fourth and finally, the ICMI standard advances the understanding of moral injury beyond solely the individual to the collective, connoting that this injury often extends far beyond the self to organizations and their leadership, again, much in concert with Shay. All in all, these are laudatory advances in our understanding of moral injury.

Definitional Drift (A Parenthetical Observation)

This brief survey of three of the most publicly utilized definitions of moral injury point to one major conclusion: *there simply is no definitive understanding of the concept.* Each version iteratively builds off the previous version, but in ways that slightly alter, and to be fair, do advance our understanding of the broad concept. However, these differences are rather more distinct than perhaps once assumed, so that between the three (and the others used in the scholarly literature which have not risen to such prominence), there is a growing sense of unclarity to what the term moral injury consistently means.[34] Indeed, each of these definitions are descriptive in nature, attempting to encapsulate what moral injury looks like rather than prescribing what it is.[35]

Generally, they collectively capture three inter-related and iterative processes: a rupture in human relationship; a resulting experience of significant emotional pain, and; a moral reflection yielding to certainty that an interior "boundary" has been crossed, whether emotional or ethical in nature. This experience of moral injury is almost always described and explored—whether in the clinical or theological discourses—from an individual perspective, while often ignoring the communal experience or effects of moral injury.[36]

Further and in my experience, this leads to a misapplication of the term with a lack of precision in context. While many clinicians and certainly many theologians may prefer this nuanced flexibility of both definition and application—seeing in it perhaps a needed fluidity—particularly in the profession of arms this is manifestly unhelpful at the strategic level of war. This is not to say that many severely traumatized warriors who have experienced moral injury have not found resonance with the concept; the opposite is certainly true. However, there is concern with divining the term's efficacy for the strategic level of war, which automatically connotes a consideration of professions, military forces, nation-states, and even transnational organizations.

In that context, a nuanced flexibility of both definition and application is unhelpful. Why so? Because unlike either the clinical or theological professions, national security professionals at this level of war need definitive clarity on and understanding of terms, because that, then, leads to a tailored understanding of both a specified context and, again ethically, a discernment of cause and effect (either past, present, or future). Put another way, strategic national security leaders make decisions about the composition and utilization of forces that require a common understanding of concepts to effectively debate possible courses of action, assess risk, approve and implement plans and orders—whether in training or operations—and then manage forces.

Moreover, and within the American tradition of civil-military relations, where such strategic national security leaders are subordinate to either elected or appointed civilians, they must have a firm grasp of such concepts to then advise those civilian leaders who will make final decisions about whether, when, and why to go to war. In that context, indeterminacy of meaning and a misapplication of terms in context is unhelpful, if not fatal.[37]

Is there a summary definition that captures all of these seemingly disparate strands of thought, each important as they are? I believe so. In 2017, I was in a doctor's office reading a veterans magazine left on a coffee table, and an article about "Moral Injury" caught my eye. The definition offered there—though not clinically nuanced, analytically verified or peer reviewed—seemed to me be one of the most comprehensive definitions of moral injury I've encountered in the literature of professionals or practitioners, and it was offered by RADM Joyce Johnson, the former Surgeon General of the United States Coast Guard. It's a descriptive summary of moral injury:

> Moral injury is not a mental illness or psychiatric diagnosis. At its base, it is an inability to address and resolve feelings of shame and guilt related to conscience, personal moral code, and spirituality. It is characterized by extreme regret and remorse days or even years after a transgression from a moral code or shared moral beliefs. The transgressing event often occurs under special circumstances, such as combat. Classic causes of moral injury include: betraying someone; being betrayed by an authority figure; perceived abusive or disproportional violence; incidents involving civilians or others; within-ranks violence; lethal force; and more generally, actions viewed as inhumane or that had terrible consequences. Moral injury can result from something a person did, neglected to do, was unable to prevent, or witnessed.[38]

Here, Johnson captures all the major strands of moral injury into a single, if not lengthy, thread.

Several features of Admiral Johnson's definition stand out: her weaving in of both the critical nouns betrayal and transgression; her appreciation of both the causal psychological responses of individuals alongside the ethical and perhaps even spiritual tension of the person; the locus within trauma; the appreciation of the military context, particularly relative to combat or the criticality of leadership; the possibility of non-combat trauma; and, the appreciation of moral agency as a precipitating factor. There is much to appreciate in this definition, whether it is known or widely used, and its broadness argues for an expansive possibility of application in many different contexts. That said, I am sanguine that even my appreciation of it will not likely broaden its acceptance amongst either of any of the major professions which respond to or analyze moral injury, but I do contend that it indicates a broadening of the use of the term and a greater (at least professional) appreciation of moral injury's multifaceted nature.

However, the fact that such a generous definition as Johnson's has not gained wider acceptance also supports my contention that a definitional miasma around moral injury clouds our understanding and application today. Candidly, here I have only several thoughts towards resolution. First, I believe it's time—particularly for the profession of arms—to coalesce around Jonathan Shay's original definition, for several reasons. As mentioned, Shay locates the nature of moral injury in military forces around the concept of betrayal, particularly by leaders in situations of immense import or threat, and so, by derivation, he rightly captures a leader imperative to consciously be self-aware, to reflect, and then to act to avoid or to prevent moral injury (as much as is possible) in his or her force. In essence, Shay raises moral injury to a leader level, adjuring that any military leader operates under a moral imperative to achieve ethical convergence in the functioning of his or her command. Indeed, he is arguing for a premium on leader integrity and convergence that, if properly employed, will mitigate against what the late Jonathan Sacks appreciated as "moral hazard," and its attendant effects on morale, fairness, and the right control of power.[39]

That said, this question of definition leads to my second question (which seems self-evident in our quest for understanding about moral injury): where is one so injured? In my pastoral work with warriors and their families, I have sensed more and more an affirmation that while moral injury is a real and very serious type of injury incurred in war, what so often warriors also are dealing with is a very real and serious type of spiritual injury, a deep wounding at the core of their being. However, and again the question forces upon our understanding a broader question centered around being. Essentially, asking where a person experiencing moral injury is, in fact, injured, entails making ontological judgments about what constitutes the nature of a person.

As a corollary, if a warrior is shot in combat, medical experts are often close to hand to diagnose the place of the bullet wound, its extent based on the ammunition used or its proximity to major organs or arteries, and even how long they then have to stabilize and evacuate that warrior before he or she is at risk of death. All of this is relative to where and how that warrior is injured, and effective combat medicine is predicated on answering this basic question.

Yet particularly in the clinical and therapeutic disciplines which dominate the care of those experiencing moral injury, there appears to be a diminishing number of perspectives willing to address this question.[40] In parsing the definitions of moral injury, one will find a swath of answers to this question which, as with agency, seem to locate the subject in abstract concepts which defy specificity: one is wounded in their mind; one is wounded in their psyche; one is wounded in their beliefs; one is wounded in their sense of self-worth; one is wounded in their emotions, one is wounded in their moral reasoning, etc.

As with the observation about clarity in definitions, this is leading to misapplication of the term moral injury to a wide swath of related but highly contextualized and differing experiences or reactions (for example, a person with generalized feelings of guilt, remorse, or sorrow often has not experienced moral injury as a violation of a core emotional belief or ethical boundary). As well, it is leading to speculative and—in my estimation—dangerous proposals from non-clinicians and therapists regarding moral injury in war. One of the most extreme is arguing for the pharmacological medication against moral injury for warriors and whole populations groups, as well as for "the weaponization of moral injury" against enemies on the battlefield.[41] Why is this so? Often, the definitions for moral injury describe more than prescribe, for whatever reason, and center the definitions based more on the feelings one experiences resulting from moral injury rather than the injury itself. Moreover, this often does not address in the least that moral injury can and does occur on a communal level beyond the individual, a point that has significant impact at the strategic level of war.

"Deeply Held" and the Power of Values, Principles, and Beliefs

How does moral injury help in this process? A critical starting point is moral and ethical self-awareness, and this as true for the individual warrior as it is for the nation that she or he serves; it holds both at the individual and at the communal levels of conscience and understanding.[42] In the tradition of American civil-military relations (which is a heritage of immense proportions from that nation to the professional militaries and democracies of the world), and as a starting point, the author is avowedly non-political. By that, as a formerly uniformed, commissioned officer, we would never venture into usurping the political authority of either the appointed or elected civilian leaders who lead, manage, and direct the United States Department of Defense and answer ultimately to the authority of the President of the United States. However, what I do wish to be is evocative in describing war as it has evolved in the past three decades and provocative about where it is evolving in roughly the next two-three decades. This is done particularly from my vantage points as an ordained clergyman, a long-serving Army chaplain, a Christian Realist in terms of geopolitical perspectives, a Just War Tradition ethicist, and a certified Army Strategist.[43] Rather than these roles being a hindrance, I believe that they can freshly inform this study—with awareness—and help to advance this discussion.

The study of moral and spiritual injury can aid us in discerning moral and ethical self-awareness and vice versa, and again, that this is as true for the individual as it is at the communal level. The reason for this is that in war, the internal woundedness of moral injury lies at the core of one's being, particularly relative to morals, ethics, decision-making, and action (or inaction), and then the attendant emotions as well as thoughts that result from that complex process. For example, sometimes when a warrior is deeply troubled by some traumatic experience to the core of their being, he or she often will not even know why they are so disturbed.

The central concept from the field of moral injury studies is that of a core value, principle, and belief being violated for a person. I term this as a boundary crossing, and it is the controlling metaphor for this book.[44] Further, in distinction from many of my colleagues in moral injury studies, this boundary crossing is not always a matter of one's emotions and dissonant feelings; rather, it can just as easily be centered around one's ethical disequilibrium and dissonant thoughts.

Essentially, moral injury is not only always centered around disordered emotions but also discordant ethical reflections, so that it is both an emotional and an ethical injury. Moreover, such a deep-seated boundary crossing encamps within one's soul, and so attains a permanence (a function of enduring over time) and pervasiveness (a function of extending to the core of one's being), truly attaining to a soul injury.[45] Again and with awareness, this is an ontological judgement here on the nature of the human person that might find little resonance within either the clinical or martial communities which dominate the contemporary discussions around moral injury. However, the growing problem of moral injury in the profession of arms occasions here a strategic inflexion point at which the world debates about what war means—or should mean—for societies and thus requires thinking about this problem in fresh ways.

Such woundedness is true not only for individuals but also for military forces, governments, nation-states, and people groups. So reflexively understood and externalized from the individual to the collective, moral injury can thus renew our understanding of the profession of arms as a values-based enterprise that again, so demarcated, can likewise be better regulated. To do so, moral injury as an interior wound of something deeply held—a boundary crossing—sharpens our self-awareness and forces us to confront the question: "What do I, or we, believe?"

Essentially, what is it that we hold so deeply—either individually or collectively—that we would consider this a value, principle, or belief which, if violated, we could categorize as the crossing of a core ethical boundary?

Emotional Dissonance and Ethical Disequilibrium

Now, here, it's not for me to identify that core boundary for each person or community—that is a subjective but critically necessary self-project. Indeed, this subjectivity is what makes moral injury untenable as a diagnosable disorder in the clinical sense, because it defies an objective standard which can be consistently applied in multiple contexts. What is important though is delineating the *process* of coming to such self-awareness; this is something worth examining in detail.

That said, the above definitions of moral injury remain somewhat incomplete as they relate to the profession of arms. For example, the ICMI definition rests only on the words 'emotions' and 'values,' but Christian ethics particularly is about far more than just values, let alone our emotions in relation to them. In essence, the definition appears to rest too much on, candidly, an American predilection towards emotional dissonance of feelings, when moral injury as a phenomenon is as much about the ethical disequilibrium produced by reflective thoughts on one's trauma as it is about how one feels about this or that experience. Is this, then, a type of American cultural hegemony towards the concept? This is a question worth exploring in a different forum than this book, but it is at least worth surfacing here. This is not to say that that emotions and feelings are not relevant to discussions about moral injury; rather, that they are incomplete in describing the full range of human experience which undergird the malady.

As an example, the adverbial phrase "deeply held" needs further exploration both in the VA and ICMI definitions. If this is particularly related to emotions and feelings, which are often transitory and contextual, then how is one's experience of moral injury then held so deeply that such an emotion or set of emotions comes to be paradigmatic for life? Feelings such as guilt, shame, anger, and remorse can become deeply embedded in one's self perspective, even to the point that such emotions become pervasive and persistent.[46] However, such emotions and feelings are almost never endemic to themselves, Instead, they relate to both one's experience and one's ongoing ethically based thoughts, reflections, questions, and assessment of one's action, inaction, or experience in each context. Emotions and feelings do not completely capture the breadth of one's experience of moral injury; ethical disequilibrium and thinking and then their accompany feelings about that reflective process are just as important to such woundedness.

Finally, this standard definition continues the pathologization of moral injury as an almost solely individual human experience. For the taxonomy of this book, it continues to locate moral injury at the tactical level of war within a person without possible application to either the operational or strategic level of war. Now again, given the roots of the term in the clinical observations of Shay, Litz, Maguen, and other leading psychiatrists, psychologists, and counselors, I am neither surprised by this nor wholly in disagreement with such a correspondence. What is lacking, however, is an acknowledgement that moral injury is not always and only to be confined to this level of experience or understanding. Rather, moral injury is just as applicable to the collective, communal experiences of military forces, professions, people groups, governments, and even nation-states. For example, that this is happening—or should happen—as a reflective process of ethical reasoning relative to both the Russo-Ukraine and Israel-Iran wars, a turn which we will make in the third chapter of this book.

For now, however, we've detailed the cause and effect of the disparate definitions of moral injury, such that there is only a general consensus on what the term means (but dependent on the definition one employs), no functional ability to consistently apply it in context (particularly for organizations whose business is the national security policymaking process), and little incorporation into our collective understanding about the malady relative to ethical disequilibrium (rather than the over focus on an individual's emotional dissonance). In sum, where has this brought us? I contend that with moral injury, at least for the profession of arms, societies are at a decision-point about that profession and its role in the future of national security.

A Crossroads for the Profession of Arms

Within existing military forces, moral injury has had several systemic impacts on the profession of arms. First, of course, is the most obvious possible correlation of moral injury to the pervasive problem of both uniformed warrior and post-uniformed veteran suicidal ideation, attempts, and completion. All the United States military services have leveraged gargantuan sums of money and human resources towards these problem within their ranks; the Veterans Administration has done the same to its client base of post-uniformed service members. Other nations have had to do the same in relation to their post-uniformed veteran classes. Statistically, in both cohorts there have been some marginal gains in reducing the per capita number of completed suicides, but the problem has remained stubbornly resistant to organizational strategies for combatting it.[47]

Although I am not making the issue of suicide in military forces or veteran populations coterminous, I think many military leaders often do just that and fail to distinguish between the two as similar but distinct problem sets (at an organizational level). Indeed, while the amount of clinical research within military forces indicates that these forces have ample evidentiary support to analyze the causes and effects of suicide within the force, there is simply not a coequal research effort within those same forces regarding moral injury.[48] However, and relative to the observation that at the strategic level of leadership within the profession of arms moral injury is being increasingly used as a term but without nuance or specificity, particularly relative to its context. I am concerned that this is leading to a general grouping of that malady with suicide, but the two are related but distinct in every way. At the strategic level of military leadership, the profession of arms must begin to differentiate and use these two terms with specificity and intentionality, or the generalized confusion about how they are related or what moral injury is will expand across the forces.

Second, I believe that moral injury has exhibited a degrading effect on tactical, operational, and strategic moral leader development and the exercise of leadership at every level of the force. J. Mark Mattox, for instance, has rightly noted (albeit prior to the Global War on Terror, so called) the corrosive effect of prolonged war on the moral fabric of fighting forces, seeing collectively a degradation in leaders' abilities to reflect on moral categories and to then wisely apply judgment in new situations demanding moral leadership.[49] This is similar to Shay's concept of moral injury producing a shrinkage of one's "moral horizon."[50] Indeed, the Department of Defense has in the last few years repeatedly and problematically had to address significant moral leadership failures at the general officer and flag ranks across all its services, not just egregious tactical level crimes as such as at Abu Ghraib.[51]

General and flag officers have exhibited an alarming trend of moral leadership failure at the strategic levels of all U.S. military forces, and this becomes a critical problem for a values-based institution such as the profession of arms. Such strategic moral leader failure degrades trust within the force to all levels of subordinate commands (as well as potentially signaling to those commands that such character or leadership failures are acceptable) and degrades trust outside the force to the profession's client, the American people. Now clearly, strategic moral leader failure and moral injury are not necessarily—as with suicide and moral injury—coterminous, but they are likely highly related. What is clear is that by 2015, the senior leadership of the Department of Defense was immensely concerned that there was indeed a persistent corrosion in the moral fiber of the strategic leadership of the military forces, and that the persistent nature of a nation at continual war by that time was a likely culprit.[52] Recall that one of the signal features of moral injury is a diminishment of one's moral horizon and an inability to achieve ethical nuance in decision-making. If such tendencies are being manifested by the senior leaders of the profession of arms, then it is at least a possible, if not likely, supposition that moral injury has somehow played a part in that outcome.

Third, the West was awakened to the moral complexity of humanitarian catastrophes during the Rwandan Genocide of 1994 and the ensuing American and European resolve to interdict such catastrophes in the NATO intervention into Bosnia-Herzegovina in 1995. Recall that a significant causal factor moral injury revolves around moral agency, and either the action or inaction of one in an ethically decisive context, particularly if in a leadership position within a military unit or force. Relative to Rwanda, this is precisely the dilemma which the appointed military leader of the United Nations force on the ground in that country, Canadian then-Brigadier General Roméo Dallaire faced at the outset of that catastrophe.

Leading a force of trained, armed, and present United Nations peacekeepers, BG Dallaire was unable to intervene to stop the genocide because he lacked the requisite political authorities from the UN to employ force in such a way; it was outside the mandate of that mission. Accordingly, of course, this contributed to the slaughter of over 500,00 to 800,000 Tutsis by the dominant Hutu majority in power (particularly militia forces), a catastrophe brought to international attention in film and media. However, and for the purposes of this book, BG Dallaire famously wrote about his leadership crisis in this situation and his subsequent experience of both deep moral injury and PTSD from this mission.[53]

At the strategic level of policymaking, former President Bill Clinton later would recall that his one signal regret in foreign affairs was not authorizing U.S. military force to intervene and stop the massacre.[54] This lead directly to the geopolitical ratification just two years later of the UN-backed Dayton Accords and deployment of a NATO peace enforcement force to Bosnia-Herzegovina to arrest the potential for another genocide in the Bosnian Civil War.[55] Thus, moral injury writ large, in part, spawned the rise of humanitarian intervention and the transnational strategic policy of the responsibility to protect as a force employment strategy, though R2P (as it has come to be known) is problematic to enact on a multinational level, to be sure.[56] Still, moral injury as a strategic problem in war catalyzed the development of recent trans-national military doctrine and planning guidelines for mass atrocity response and prevention efforts.[57] If this tragedy in Rwanda illumines anything beyond our sorrow at such immense loss of life, it is that the strategic risk of moral injury in future nation-state war is monumental indeed.

Fourth and finally, moral injury as a phenomenon has galvanized national will in the United States to empathically respond to warriors and veterans, leading to vast economic investments into care for post-war veterans and pensioners.[58] Perhaps to assuage a type of national guilt over the treatment of Vietnam veterans in the 1970s, beginning with the Reagan Administration's championing of a Vietnam Veterans Memorial in Washington, DC, a catalyzed political will began to take hold to separate American social treatment of the war's veterans from political assessments about the war. This, in turn, fueled a larger social approbation of veterans as a social class, a phenomenon further accentuated by the American-led coalition's battlefield success in the first Persian Gulf War, titled Operation Desert Storm.

In short, since formal end of the Vietnam War in 1975, American social attitudes about its veterans have exponentially improved, as has the public's trust of the military as a social institution charged with maintaining the nation's security. Though some have rightly questioned whether this has, in turn, produced an over emphasis within the military and veteran bureaucracies on pursuing the monetization of woundedness and that the fiscal care of veterans as a social class has reached excessive proportions of discretionary spending within the federal budget, this trend shows no abatement.[59] Derivatively, this should highlight and therefore increase a national focus on moral injury related to the profession of arms. However, what this has not done is to raise to a broader social level of discussion some of the more definitive questions with which we've attended in this chapter. Moreover, what it has also not done is to raise to that same social level of discussion related questions which are just as important about the nature of such woundedness related to the nature of persons serving in uniform. This has placed the profession of arms at an ontological crossroads, to be sure, and so to that task, we now turn.

2

BOUNDARY CROSSING: SPIRITUAL INJURY

The Political and Ontological Context and Problem

War is the one of the most anti-human of experiences. It degrades, rends, and tears at people both in body and soul. It degrades, rends, and tears at human societies in our familial and collective relationships and in the created order. Yet despite its destructiveness, war remains an enduring and necessary reality because it checks unrestrained evil, corrects injustice, and restores, if only temporarily, a semblance of social cohesion and stability. In Christian theology, while war may destroy the body, it cannot destroy the soul—that which is created and sustained by God for eternity is beyond even the catastrophic power of war to ultimately destroy (Matt. 10:28a). Nevertheless, along with all citizens of good will and communal commitment, Christians can neither ignore the ways in which war injures warriors and their families nor ignore their responsibility on behalf of Christ to respond to others with genuine *caritas*. In essence, for Christians, there is a cost to living Jesus' ethic of love, paid, in part, through action.[1] Exploring that cost and the landscape of suffering in war as spiritual injury is the exercise of this chapter.

Yet this is, admittedly, very difficult in the present social context. Why so? First, as previously alluded to, there has been a corrosive diminution of religious perspective into American national security policymaking in the past forty or so years. I am not referring here to the social importance of religion in America, its confessional trends in one or another direction, or in its relative impact on American electoral politics. Rather, I am specifically referring to what many observers have repeatedly noted: the United States government does not routinely incorporate an understanding of religion, its histories, its movements, its leaders, its issues, etc. into its deliberations about formulating, pursuing, and achieving strategic political ends, ways, and means.

This generally arises from an institutional heuristic in the career national security professions (whether in the diplomatic, informational, military, economic, financial, intelligence, or law enforcement instruments of national power) against incorporating any appreciation of religion or its related issues into institutional decision-making.[2] Whether from a latent anti-religious bias against or simple professional ignorance of religion, this seems self-evidently true. As Tom Farr has noted from his U.S. diplomatic career (and which he later extrapolates to the broader national security establishment):

> Madeleine Albright once wrote that diplomats of her era were trained to stay away from religion. Well, that religion avoidance syndrome has diminished somewhat in recent years, but it has not entirely disappeared from Foggy Bottom...I'm not suggesting that our foreign policy should be Christian. I am suggesting that an aggressive secularism at the State Department has handicapped our foreign policy of advancing international religious freedom...our foreign policy elites no longer understand the true meaning and value of religious freedom to America, let alone to other nations. Their decisions are tactical and, in my view, deeply mistaken.[3]

However, there is a second reason this issue of a warrior's being is so potentially anathema to professional consideration today. Principally, this is because venturing into the realm of spiritual injury necessarily enjoins one to make ontological judgments about the nature of human personhood and potentially to the nature of a person's relationship to the Divine. This is categorically an area which many secular philosophers, ethicists, and clinical and martial experts in moral injury have studiously sought to avoid.

However, arising from my military pastoral experience, and more importantly because of the frustration I've heard many warriors and families voice that the totality of their being was not being considered. This subject cannot be dismissed, for the human pain, suffering, and tragedy of war will not allow for such a move. On this point, I am reminded of the words of General George C. Marshall, then Chief of Staff of the U.S. Army, in a speech to Trinity College in Hartford, Connecticut just prior to the entrance of America into World War II. When asked to speak on the role of technology in future war, Marshall categorically enjoined:

> It is true, as the daily press points out, that we are applying all of American energy, ingenuity and genius we can mobilize, to the task of equipping our new Army with the most modern and efficient weapons in the world—and in ever-increasing quantity. That is our responsibility and you expect us to meet it. But underlying all, the effort back of this essentially material and industrial effort is the realization that the primary instrument of warfare is the fighting man. All of the weapons with which we arm him are merely tools to enable him to carry out his mission…We want all of these to be available in such quantity and quality that they will be sustaining factors when it comes to a consideration of the soldier's spirit. The soldier's heart, the soldier's spirit, the soldier's soul, are everything. Unless the soldier's soul sustains him he cannot be relied on and will fail himself and his commander and his country in the end.[4]

The question today is whether Marshall's observations still hold? I believe they do so, but that to address both his concern and the policymaking void which I've outlined requires a fresh appraisal on our part of spiritual injury and, conversely with Marshall, spiritual resilience in war.

Spiritual Injury in War Today—Two Questions

To begin and as with the concept of moral injury, there are two questions which seem to naturally lend themselves to our inquiry:

1. What is the Definition of Spiritual Injury?
2. Where is One Wounded through Spiritual Injury?

To review, much has been written in the past decades or more on the types of "woundedness" warriors suffer in combat, including physical, mental, emotional, and even moral injury. However, though U.S. joint forces are pursuing strategies for increasing "spiritual resilience" in warriors with an eye toward improving future training and operational readiness, the force has failed to explore a warrior's spiritual injury in combat and its debilitating, life-long effects (including for a warrior's family).[5] I want to attend to this oversight by defining spiritual injury as related to, yet separate from, moral injury. Later in this chapter, I will delineate eight specific markers of spiritual injury (in the present study, relative to war) and suggest how clergy, chaplains, clinicians, and concerned laypersons may identify and begin to respond to these wounds. Ironically, and yet in hope, I argue that trauma in war aids us in identifying the markers of spiritual injury and in authentically living a redemptive ethic of self-emptying love for others.[6]

To review, however, since the close of the Vietnam War, the fields of psychiatry, psychology, and pastoral counseling have grown incredibly nuanced in their understanding of the complexity of trauma in war. Clinicians and scholars have helped map what moral injury looks like in warriors, including identifying markers such as pervasive guilt and shame, feelings of being beyond forgiveness, the development of a hopeless nihilism, social distance from community and creation, a diminished reflective capacity to render morally nuanced distinctions between right and wrong, and a degraded or corroded ability to exercise leadership, particularly to exhibit or develop tactical, operational, and strategic moral leadership.[7]

Beyond the impact on individuals, our deepened awareness of moral injury has helped spawn the rise of humanitarian intervention and the trans-national ideology of the responsibility to protect; has, more recently, catalyzed the development of military doctrine such as that for mass atrocity response operations; and has galvanized national will to empathically respond to warriors and veterans, leading to immense economic investments into care for postwar veterans and pensioners. Finally, while it shouldn't be lost amid these martial examples that moral injury has relevance beyond the military, it's not incidental that moral injury is most closely linked to combat trauma.[8]

This noted, in more than a quarter century of pastoral work with warriors and their families, I have sensed a growing affirmation that warriors suffer also from another kind of soul wound, which I've specified as a spiritual injury, that is related to but distinct from moral injury as clinically understood. Coupling my observations and insights with those of fellow chaplains of all the services, we may go so far as to state that a warrior and family may often be suffering the effects of a spiritual injury without suffering the effects of moral injury. This distinction of moral and spiritual injury, though yet parallel, is intended to emphasize, if not reclaim, a basic, ontological understanding of human personhood that is consistent with a theological understanding of the created order and God's design for humanity.[9] How so? As Martin Thornton notes, "Fundamental to the Biblical doctrine of man is the principle of total integration. Human beings cannot be split up into parts and 'faculties'; body and spirit form an indissoluble unity."[10] I propose that the addition of spiritual injury, as opposed to moral injury alone, is necessary to treat warriors and their families as precisely such indissoluble unities; that is, as whole persons who are inextricably bound to their communal relationships, particularly their family systems and the profession of arms.[11]

Thus to our first question, *how do we define spiritual injury?* Perhaps surprisingly, several definitions of spiritual injury are latent in the professional discourse amongst clinicians, pastoral theologians, chaplains and clergy. The first definition which principally arose in the literature is that of G. E. Berg (as cited by Lindsay Carey), who defined spiritual injury as "...our response to an event caused by self, or an event beyond our control, that damages our relationship with God, self and others, and alienates us from that which gives meaning to our lives."[12] Carey notes that based on Berg's original definition that the term *spiritual injury* actually predates that of *moral injury* in the professional discourse. That said, Berg's concept was nascent and constrained, and as Carey further notes, was expanded upon by J. E. Fuson in 2013:

> The term "spiritual injury" is used to describe the condition where one's spiritual identity is in question. The individual suffering from spiritual injury has difficulty understanding how his or her view of faith, spirituality, relationship with God, and God's involvement in one's life can be true given the horrific experiences observed. A person suffering from spiritual injury doesn't have answers to the questions related to the trauma he or she has experienced, is unsure how to resolve this tension and find the answers, and/or may be doubting that God is trustworthy.[13]

While these two definitions, which are admittedly less well-known than that or moral injury, are helpful, they are limited in scope. Both are helpful in that, first and foremost, they acknowledge the ontological divide which predicates this chapter, that is that people are unitive both in body and soul. Second, they further acknowledge that this finds expression in an ongoing relationships with both God and others, and that spiritual injury places these relationships either in tension or in outright jeopardy, due to the potential severity of one's trauma. Finally, particularly Fuson centers his understanding of this malady on the critical self-understanding of identity, and particularly for one who is deeply formed in that Divine-human relationship, the potential or actual rupture of that relationship further threatens one's sense of self as well, and how that is then framed in a derivative epistemological doubt about God's ability to be trusted. These are significant and important aspects which commend both these definitions.

Even so, they are somewhat nascent in form and not broadly applied in the range and scope of human life after trauma. Berg's definition only alludes to the epistemological risk of spiritual injury, and while Fuson expands on this, his chosen context is to explore this relative to a Christian pastoral theological response through employing a biblically-based counselling modality. This, perhaps, helpful and appropriate for both Christian pastoral theologians, pastors, counsellors, and chaplains and for their confessionally Christian adherents, but what of those not from within this tradition? Can the broader field of Christian theology provide a framework for understanding spiritual injury that can be flexibly applied to non-Christian religious or counselling professionals and to non-Christian persons suffering the soul wounds of trauma?

A warrior suffers spiritual injury in their soul, which is the core of their being. Comparatively, and responding both to these preceding definitions as well as to the major definitions of moral injury surveyed in the prior chapter, I propose an updated definition, further delineated by eight derivative markers.[14] I define spiritual injury as:

> A person's deep wounding of the soul arising from life-altering trauma, misbalancing one's core sense of self and threatening one's relationships to others and God.

What are some relative (and certainly to be debated) strengths of this definition? First, by defining spiritual injury as has been done above, I am first and foremost theologically attending to the ontological nature of the human person, incorporating a unitive understanding of how this injury not only directly impacts the soul but also derivatively impacts the sense of self at the core of one's being (perhaps located within the mind [a philosophically debated concept, to be sure] and in many theological traditions, then, a function of the created human body). What do I mean by this? Here, we borrow from psycho-social understandings of the self as reasoning, understanding, reflection, memory, judgment, will, etc., and certainly how a person links these understandings to subsequent emotional expressions such as the capacity for love, joy, hope, faith, etc. In essence, and borrowing from my critique of moral injury as being overly focused on the damage to human emotions and feelings and not attentive enough to disequilibrium in human ethical reasoning and reflection, I want this definition to provide for this possibility without prescribing it. This definition is person-centered rather than event-centered, and grammatically identifies an individual as the subject.

Second, I anchor the definition on a broad, admittedly inchoate phrase of life-altering trauma. With this, I am attempting to delineate spiritual injury by its severity deriving specifically from trauma, though admittedly this remains somewhat opaque. Still, I trust most people at least have some generalized notion that trauma is an experience on the person (perhaps, à la moral injury that one did, one failed to do, or one had done to them), that somehow impacts the soul in a catalytic way. Theologically and perhaps extrapolated, perhaps trauma can be seen as a subset of sin, which Brian Powers notes is, "...a force that pervades and infects humanity, poisoning its moral capacities in insidious ways." [15] Trauma has the power to become both pervasive to the core of one's being and persistent across the whole of one's life if left unchecked. This is so for individuals as well as communal groups.[16] Here, I am attempting to move both our understandings of moral and spiritual injury away from generalized emphases on feelings only, and by so qualifying spiritual injury at least, the totality of how such injury can only genuinely arise from a significant, life-altering traumatic event.

Towards Clarity: Eight Markers of Spiritual Injury

Seeking to achieve the above end of delineating between spiritual and moral injucy, let me outline a theological moral framework for understanding spiritual injury, particularly relative to war. Based upon the definition given above, spiritual injury may be demarcated by eight distinctive markers:

1. The Loss of God in Relationship (Abandonment and Estrangement)—The first and most prevalent distinctive marker is when a warrior struggles over whether he or she has irreparably been separated from God. For warriors, as with moral injury, such questioning may arise from guilt over actions taken or not taken in combat but not exclusively so; indeed, the trauma suffered may have been inflicted upon them by another. For many, simply living through and surviving the experience of combat can produce such searching because war as an experience tends to strain personal assumptions, challenge lightly or deeply held beliefs, and force even healthy persons to seek stronger connections with God, or to abandon God in trauma's wasting wake. Expressed as a function of relationship, this can lead to a sense that God has somehow abandoned them, or at the very least, that they are estranged from God and so somehow unworthy or unable to participate in a Divine-human relationship. In my military pastoral experience, this is the first and most evident marker that a warrior is suffering spiritual injury, even if they lack the

language to express the idea. Still, what they often can and will be able to capture is a deep, unmovable sense of loss... real loss...of their worthiness for or God's willingness to receive them back into relationship.

2. Doubt of God's Providence and/or Sovereignty (Loss of Divine Control and Resulting Injustice)—As war can, and often does, produce a significant existential crisis for the warrior that is framed in questions of ultimate meaning, this is particularly so in his or her relationship both to others and to God. A Soldier once pointedly asked me after witnessing a horrific scene of carnage in combat, "Chaplain, what happened today, did God take the day off?" That question epitomizes the existential struggle some warriors face after a fight as they reflect on what they saw, heard, tasted, smelled, and touched in combat. War is visceral, yet ethereal, and can often cause warriors to challenge their own beliefs about how, or if, God was in control of a fight, and why He allowed such carnage to occur. Death, chance, horrific injury, and the social wastage of combat can produce overwhelming questions about God's sovereign omniscience (unlimited knowledge), omnipresence (unlimited presence), and omnipotence (unlimited power). Conversely, with an enhanced understanding of one's power of moral agency, some drift into an unhealthful if not unholy sense of imperviousness and power, a dynamic that can lead to externalized heinous war crimes and genocide. However, short of these extremes, at the very least, many warriors exhibiting this marker often devolve into an angry bitterness at the injustice of war and cannot frame any type of healthful moral meaning around either its outcome of their participation in it. Such existential doubts and searching for moral meaning must never be facilely dismissed, for resolving them is critical to life.[17]

3. Encountering Evil (Theodicy, Suffering, and Sorrow)—Evil is real; many have seen it, heard it, felt it, smelled it, tasted it, and touched it, particularly in war. Relentlessly driven by unyielding hate and a thirst for our destruction, it seeks to consume every one of us (Mark 5:2–9). One of the most ancient, compelling accounts of theodicy (the presence and power of evil in creation) is, of course, from the book of Job. In it, the text invites us to take seriously that though evil is real, and God allows suffering to happen (even to an externally righteous man like Job), it is limited in scope, duration, and existential effect. (Job 1:6–12) However, many warriors encountering evil and its attendant suffering on others are often consumed by it, overwhelmed far beyond simple empathetic pity or compassion by its seeming indiscriminate senselessness. Moreover, how they experience evil through the suffering of themselves or others often shakes them to the core of their being, deep within their soul. This can arrest appropriate moral emotions, particularly sorrow, which should be a warrior's normal response to the suffering of war. Conversely and that qualification noted, for many sorrow subsequently becomes an overwhelming and overarching paradigm of life. If such sorrow is left unchecked, it can envelop the soul and hold it hostage to past experience. Here, suffering can make manifest the old truism: "Some soldiers leave the battlefield but the battlefield never leaves them." Such a marker of spiritual injury is allied with moral injury in that the trauma can arrest mental cognition, compromise reasoning, and short-circuit memory. However, unlike moral injury, suffering and sorrow here connotes a spiritual weight that anchors the warrior to an ever-present past in a grieving process without end that comes to dominate everyday life, present reality, and certainly any capacity for future hope. Evil may indeed be limited in scope, duration, and effect, but for many warriors, its weight becomes temporally and eternally oppressive.

4. The Challenge of Forgiveness (Of the Self, from Others and from God)—Especially related to suffering is the human need for forgiveness. This is something apart from simply reconciling negative moral emotions, real as are these emotional responses to trauma. While clinical therapeutic practice rightly helps a warrior explore past events and his or her moral agency or decision-making within them, forgiveness is a far different prospect. Sometimes warriors suffering spiritual injury need more than just a psychological exploration leading to a justification of their role in combat; they really do need to be forgiven for what they did or did not do. Notwithstanding that in contemporary democracies military forces are often composed only of highly skilled professionals, even such warriors can find that the moral and spiritual consequences of their volunteerism are immense and repetitive, and consequently so is their internal woundedness. The challenge of forgiveness, then, becomes iterative and compounding. Even the most morally well-formed warriors are human beings who, even with serving with moral probity, often both want and need forgiveness for their actions or attitudes in combat that do not fully align with the deeply held values, principles, and beliefs required of their faith. Such forgiveness cannot only come from within the self but must also be received in community, perhaps even through religious rites of either confession, penance, absolution, or atonement. Clergy and military chaplains with the referential authority of serving in God's stead from within their faith tradition (or from the wider community) may be the focal touchpoint of declaring such forgiveness when no other voice can be heard within one's soul.

5. Wrestling with Paralyzing Doubt (Questioning Foundational Faith and Truth Claims)—Combat has a way of compelling a warrior to reassess often long-held claims to truth and faith

related to their individual confessional beliefs. Again, this process is not necessarily to be avoided as it can be a potential pathway to healing, especially when undertaken in the care of a capable guide. That said, the effective guide—whether a pastoral theologian, counselor, chaplain, clergy person, or simply a wise friend—will have to refrain from aggressively challenging a warrior's crisis of doubt, their faltering faith, or the validity of their questions, however blasphemous, trite, or beside-the-point they may appear to anyone else. Warriors will often have viscerally intuited war in such a way that previously accepted tenants of their faith may be called into question in ways that are sometimes surprising, but which represent genuine spiritual crisis. For instance, when one has seen a friend so completely disintegrated through the force of a massive IED so that there are no remains to be recovered, ideas such as the bodily resurrection can suddenly seem illogical if not disrespectful to their memory. Indeed, such tenets of faith can now be catalysts for pain-filled, deeply urgent doubt. Left unaddressed, such doubt can advance to a moral paralysis, arresting any further healthy growth in reflection and reasoning on values, principles, and beliefs which are necessary for healthful maturation, the restoration of relationships, and even for life itself. Alternatively, the warrior may project his or her own self-doubt onto God, turning it into a cause for Divine self-judgment. As well and rather than admitting and locating this doubt within the self, the warrior might then defend against the Divine condemnation by turning his or her own self-doubt into a critique of God. Here is an important potential vein for treatment, in that clinicians, chaplains, and clergy can recognize such projection and gently turn the warrior back toward a self-understanding and acceptance of existential doubt. Such doubt, then, becomes a healthy (and not fatal) part of the life of the soul. On the other hand, failure to treat such doubt can become debilitating, in that a warrior might come to an unhealthy point of stasis, in which perpetual, existential doubt is simply the permanent state of the soul. The cost of this might be never recovering a sense of God's abiding peace or the transcendent hope that marks a healthy posture for the soul.

6. The Challenge of Restoration and Reconciliation (Inability to Extend in Communal Healing and Reintegration)—When a warrior returns to his or her family from combat and feels that they have either no warrant or ability to share their suffering (though the family as a system often intuits the warrior's spiritual injury and longs to participate in the healing), then the spiritual injury of suffering within that soul can become extended into the closest of family relationships. Left unchecked, this can become for the family system a permanent and perhaps even debilitating woundedness. Resultingly, when the warrior internationalizes anger, this can then lead to externalized rage, which has been a part of warrior character from the age of Achilles to the present day. This rage can further be expressed in a desire for evening the score, "paying back" the enemy, and seeking vengeance. However, these can be potentially healthy signs in a trauma-afflicted warrior. I say this because when the warrior externalizes such anger and rage, however disproportionate, it is often proof of a still functioning soul. For example, while a desire for justice is a right response to injustice, it is a virtue that, like all virtues, can be knocked off balance, but it is better than spiritual apathy or indifference, what the Greeks termed *acedia*. Still, theological questions remain over whether and how war is right and just and whether actions conducted within combat are geared toward restoration of justice and, through that, peace (perhaps in the long-term through reconciliation of warring parties or individual enemies). The need for restoration and reconciliation are powerful antidotes to externalized

anger and rage and are themselves expressions of a search for justice from combat, an attempt at moral meaning-making from war. Warriors need to rationally think through both how and why they went to war and how and what they did during war to achieve this sense of meaning to the experience. Without it, restoration and reconciliation become citizens of a distant land to which the warrior longs to go but feels they cannot, with anger and rage as unwanted but ever-present companions.

7. The Loss of Identity, Meaning, and Purpose (Both Temporal and Eternal and Ultimately a Question of Being)—This set of ideas is perhaps one of the more evident markers of spiritual injury and, collectively, can often be summed up by the warrior in the inquiry, "Who am I now, what does this experience mean for me, and what am I to do with it in the future?" The process in play is really one of integrating the experience of war into one's sense of personhood. This process very often centers around the soul and one's relationship to God, as God is typically the unspoken object of the above questions, even if only tacitly acknowledged in the questioning. That said, this exchange is imperative for the holistic healing of the warrior; war must be integrated into the soul. One cannot permanently hold it apart or aloof from oneself; it must be seen as a part of a healthfully reframed identity. Not accomplished, the warrior never moves past the question of identity to either finding meaning or purpose for war. Therefore, a thorough exploration of identity, meaning, and purpose relative to combat experience, especially traumatic experience, is a painful yet necessary process of faith seeking understanding, to place it in Anselmian terms. After war, this search is a soul's attempt to place the totality of spiritual injury into a type of ontological context.

8. The Tension of Temporal and Eternal Life (Delinking Present Experience to Redemptive Faith and a Hope)— Lastly, warriors suffering from spiritual injury are often almost devoid of any meaningful social connections or relationships with others. This leads to another personal marker of spiritual injury, and that is an inability to live from a posture of despair to any conceptualization of, let alone hope in, in eternal life. Perhaps attenuated by the post-modern context, many warriors already have little (if any) understanding of the need to see themselves as eternal beings worthy of and possibly destined for eternal life in God, much less to draw a temporal hope from that belief. Indeed, a persistent nihilistic attitude marks the present generations who serve in the modern armed forces, where warriors without combat trauma see themselves only in the present moment, whose decisions are devoid of life-long, let alone eternal, import. Add to such a perspective the trauma of combat, and such warriors are even less likely to understand, let alone appropriate, an existential hope in their possibility for eternal life in God. Still, not only is such a hope possible, often it is the most potent antidote to the immense suffering of either moral or, certainly, spiritual injury. This should be a motivating catalyst for communities of faith to embody the possibility of such hope to warriors imprisoned in their trauma. Especially within a congregation, a warrior should see that their suffering is not an end unto itself but a means to an end, a type of redemptive suffering which has existential purpose. Lacking this, however, warriors (as all victims of trauma) often remain locked inside their present experience and are unable to even conceive of a subsequent linkage between faith and existential hope.[18] Sadly, during the recent conflicts in both Afghanistan and Iraq which marked many Western nations, there is little visceral evidence that Christians of any major communion have genuinely attempted to reach spiritually injured warriors, in order to

welcome them into (and find healing amongst) "the community of the saints."

In sum, spiritual injury is a malady that can be both defined and demarcated but one which is related to, yet distinct from, moral injury. Whereas the latter is principally focused on treating the emotional and mental wounds of war regnant in the mind, the former is concerned with treating the spiritual wounds of war regnant in the soul. As both the mind as a part of the body and the soul as a metaphysical reality form an indissoluble unity within each person, the two maladies appear difficult to tease apart. However, the preceding markers may help delineate the two maladies, and offer suggestions to collaborative, inter-disciplinary approaches to healing for both clinicians and clergy alike in attending to victims of trauma. Thus, the two are not mutually exclusive but mutually reinforcing, and this is true both for the individual and the communal levels of being, as we shall see in the concluding chapter.

Of the Power of Family Systems

A final word, however, is in order regarding spiritual injury. Following Jonathan Shay's emphasis on moral injury as played out in the *themis* of a military formation (so the close-knit ethos of units predicated on relationships), this points to a reality which has yet to be detailed in any serious manner, but which necessarily deserves elucidation in this chapter. Spiritual injury particularly is very much felt and experienced in the family systems of wounded warriors.[19] How so? Based on my military pastoral experience, I count at least three significant points for reflection.

First, the warrior's woundedness very quickly becomes the family system's woundedness. As mentioned, upon redeployment from combat and reintegration into the family system, there is often a period of somewhat tense readjustment. For the warrior suffering from lingering spiritual injury, the family may sense this but not quite know how to address it. Why is this so? Partly this is due to the mechanics of day-to-day living. Roles have been reapportioned, authorities have been redistributed (for a parent, often fusing both mother and father responsibilities into the remaining parent), goals have been renegotiated, etc., and the one parent has been singularly absent. Even not counting marital relationships with children, this is true for couples without children and for single warriors who return from war suffering from spiritual injury, the latter often returning to their families of origin with the same distancing dynamics, a reality brilliantly captured by Ernest Hemingway in his short story entitled "Soldier's Home."[20] Notwithstanding this, if this spiritual woundedness is deeply entrenched within the warrior, the family—though now often trying to maintain a respectful distance—will quickly both intuit this woundedness and internalize it into the system. Should such spiritual injury remain buried in the warrior, it will remain buried in the family system until resolution in the one affords resolution in the other.

Second, however, and reflexively, this affords a unique opportunity for healing, in that the family system holds the power to both reflect to the warrior his or her woundedness and to become the vessel though which healing may occur. What this means is that when, in due course, the embedded spiritual injury of the warrior resists all other efforts at being surfaced, the family system may become a type of "mirror" in which the warrior sees her or his woundedness in the family's woundedness. Even if the family system does not rise to a level of group consciousness about its now-internalized spiritual injury, they may powerfully reflect this back to the warrior in such a way that confronts him or her with their own causal woundedness. Additionally, however, and when all other efforts at healing may have reached an impasse, the family system may offer the spiritually wounded warrior a non-threatening context by which they can receive the healing that remains otherwise elusive.

All of this, of course, is predicated on the family system being in healthy tension with one another, moderated by factors such as genuine love for one another, generally balanced stasis in the system, healthy parental roles and authorities, shared commitments to individual and collective growth, effective communication patters, and the like. However, and given the lengthy time horizon which reintegration into even healthy post-combat family systems can take, effective and complete healing from spiritual woundedness may be a project of some years.[21]

Finally, however, a powerful differentiation of the family system relative to spiritual injury is in order. For those families who do successfully navigate both a warrior's and the family's experience of spiritual injury, this has the potential to become a defining part of the family system's story about itself and attempt at meaning making around war.

In Christian taxonomy, we might say that such a cycle of injury and recovery can become a foundational element of the family system's testimony about both itself and about God working in and through the family. In essence, this experience becomes witness to the trialogical nature of communal spiritual injury and recovery process that includes the warrior, the family system, and God. So powerful can such meaning making be that, as with Bowen, this becomes a new paradigm for family collective self-understanding and for augmented individual identities for each constituent member.

If each person is allowed to remain healthfully self-differentiated, this shapes a new "I/We/God" identity that can renew both individual and collective senses of meaning and purpose to spiritual injury. In this way, even in the face of manifestly horrific trauma and its derivative impact, redemptive suffering occurs which, rather than being senseless and purposless, comes to be seen as pathways that have led to renewed growth. However, a point of caution is in order here: again, and following Bowen, this may become a project of one generation to another (Ex. 34:6–7a). Essentially, this cycle of both spiritual injury and healing may take decades to effect and be a project which calls thus for steadfast commitment of each family member to their own recovery as well as the recovery of the family system over many decades. Still, the witness of countless warriors and families coming home from war is that such potential is possible in rich, hope-filled ways which could previously have been unimagined.

A Crossroads for Communities of Faith

In response to this phenomenon of family systems embodying moral and spiritual injury, the profession of arms is at a crossroads with these problems, I further contend that our nation's communities of faith are at a similar crossroads, though perhaps ignorantly so. For instance, one might rightly ask about the collective responses of, at least in the American context, the major denominations and faith traditions resident within the body politic. If spiritual injury, particularly, is such a collective malady and so vital a threat to the life and health of the almost 1.4 million uniformed souls of America's military services, not counting their millions of family members, should not the nation's churches, synagogues, mosques, and parishes be coordinating either inter or intra-denominational response efforts?

To the contrary, in my estimation. As I have written previously relative to moral and spiritual injury, "I suggest broadly that… national denominational communities and faith traditions have unconsciously abetted and exacerbated the problem."[22] If we consider religion and religious traditions at the strategic level of society, then as organizations regnant within the culture, our major denominations and faith traditions have evidenced little to no coordinated, resourced, and consistent strategies for addressing either moral or spiritual injury in their pews. Moreover, most neither evidence any type of programmatic or systematized concern for warriors and their families at the local level nor any interest or ability to influence national security policymaking at the national level.

I believe that most of the nation's major denominations and faith traditions have treated such warriors and their families as congregational ghosts—here one day and gone the next—and abetted strategic moral and spiritual injury by adopting the cultural bias from the society around them about the nation's profession of arms, to wit: "the nation's security is not our concern, as we have standing military forces to deal with that." Hence the damning indictment of Ed Tick, that he has rightly said such faith traditions keep warriors and families "out of sight, out of mind" and thus unintentionally support the broader chasm between the profession of arms and the body politic. In his words, "We do not help survivors rebuild dignity and rediscover inner peace."[23]

As suggested earlier, there are three possibilities at the strategic religious level for addressing this shortcoming. They are for America's major denominations and faith traditions to; 1) develop religious education curricula for forming their confessional adherents as morally well-formed and integrated citizens aimed at supporting the common good of the body politic; 2) develop comprehensive programs for the sending and receiving of warriors to deployed service, and the pastoral care of their families during such specific times of separation, and; 3) develop a corporate vocation for the pastoral care and support of post-uniformed veterans and their families once such service is concluded, particularly attuned to the ever-present threat of suicide amongst this particular cohort.[24] This is a minimal collective response to be undertaken from an ecclesiastically internal posture, but there is much more that can be done.

First, and again, from the strategic level for major denominations and faith traditions across America, the problems of moral and spiritual injury amongst the profession of arms are national problems requiring national solutions. This necessarily implies that at this level, there should be coordinated and consistent cross-denominational coordination of planning and programs to support warriors and their families experiencing such woundedness. In essence, these bodies must mirror with and for each other what they are doing internally for their own confessional adherents. Done on the local level, such cross-religious efforts habitually bring about reconciliation and renewal; done at the national level, it's a reasonable expectation that this would spread the leaven of these graces across the body politic.

Second, these maladies of moral and spiritual injury are not confined to one nation's shores. Indeed, and from my recent experience working with both the military chaplains and national religious leaders of dozens of nations, these are now trans-national problems, though often attenuated by each nation's contexts, particularly their histories, values, political systems, and roles for their military forces.[25] So, just as America's major denominations and faith traditions must look inwardly down and in towards their own adherents and outwardly left and right towards other confessions' adherents, they must also expand this effort to link arms, as it were, with perhaps their fellow believers in other countries. Indeed, the challenges of moral and spiritual injury can and should spur an inter-religious dialogue across confessional lines and even international boundaries to find mutually reinforcing and beneficial solution sets that strengthen global religious peoples and their nation-states. As many will readily observe, the problems of war in one nation often have a direct, tangible, and lasting impact on many other nations, so coordinating response begets the international interest to ameliorate war's impact and set the conditions for just, lasting, and stable peace are in every nation's interests.

Third, the major denominations and faith traditions of America must reappropriate the social vocation of moral and ethical faith-based advisement to the national command authority. Indeed, the way the American national security policymaking process is now formed, such denominations and faith traditions have no day-to-day part…at all. Some might perhaps see this as a good in support of maintaining a healthy distance between church and state, so to speak. However, the reality is that now, this is no longer a healthfully maintained distance but a complete estrangement, in which the nation's major denominations and faith traditions have neither the offices, systems, processes, nor trained expertise to even minimally comment on major national questions regarding national security policymaking, let alone major national ethical questions regarding when, where, why, how, and to what purpose the nation should employ the force of arms.

To call this a strategic religious neglect is an understatement; it is in fact a strategic religious dereliction of social duty. Some bright spots are seen on the margins, as previously mentioned, particularly relative to the nation's Department of State, but again, these are not integrated into the national security policymaking process. America needs its major denominations and faith traditions to reclaim this corporate national vocation, because the reason and reflection of faith rightly has a role in sustaining a healthy body politic, or as Martin Marty has termed it, wisely exercising "theologies of public order."[26]

Why is the so important? Well again, war is quickly becoming a trans-national problem set which requires coordinated national and transnational solutions. As we are about to see, our recent history indicates this truth and should sound the tocsin about the risk of strategic moral and spiritual injury and future war.

3

BOUNDARY THREATS: CURRENT WAR

Afghanistan and the Rupture of Trust

Has modern war, particularly the massively destructive regional conflicts of both Russo-Ukraine and Israel-Iran, changed either the nature or character of war beyond recognition?[1] Does technology, for instance, obviate that war remains a human-centered phenomenon, either in its initiation, prosecution, resolution, or potential for reconciliation? Is war now solely a province of nation-states, with potentially a return of existential risk to humanity through a return to use of chemical, biological, radiological, or nuclear weapons, as opposed to the counterinsurgencies of the past two decades?[2]

The reasons these questions disturb us so deeply now are now at least three-fold, as geopolitically, the world's major democracies and peoples are: 1) suspicious at best, if not forlorn, that a peaceful outcome to either of these intractable conflicts can be found; 2) nervous that these two conflicts will morph into even wider regional conflicts, if not global ones, and; 3) anxious that these types of conflict—and their attendant changes either in the nature or character of war—are threatening harbingers of future wars that could existentially threaten our respective nation-states and the international rules-based order.[3]

Although presidential policy articulation for any administration is of immense importance in the national security policymaking process is, it is not total in its ability to healthfully shape and achieve a balance between ends, ways, and means in that process.

Indeed, what is just as vital—it not more so—and problematic in the American context, given our change of presidential administrations every four years, is the struggle to achieve policy consistency. No recent case study illustrates that more than the ill-considered, precipitous, and shambolic American ceding of the battlefield to the Taliban in Afghanistan in the fall of 2021. Before we attend to how the current wars in both Russo-Ukraine and Israel-Iran are reshaping our understanding of moral and spiritual injury in war, we must linger on that cataclysmic event because it shapes how we think of these conflicts.

The September 2021 rapid capitulation of the Afghan government, military and police forces to the Taliban justly produced a well-occasioned assessment of the United States' strategic role in how the conflict ended. For service members of all nation's militaries who were "on the ground" there, lingering questions about their own moral judgment and/or culpability, perceptions of lasting impact and change, and even assessments of their continuing professional commitment may resonate for years. Indeed, paired with a leader's self-reflection of how such questions must be answered to his or her own warriors who served in combat—or worse, to the families of those who fell in battle—the United States and global allies have an immense challenge of strategic moral and perhaps spiritual injury now latent in the post-Afghanistan professional military class.

Vital to our understanding, however, is a parallel strategic concept which very much needs deliberation regarding future *ante bellum* preparation for war and *ad bellum* decisions to initiate war, and that is the notion of strategic betrayal. If we incorporate Jonathan Shay's paradigmatic elucidation of tactical leadership betrayal in the Vietnam War, we can discern three initial trajectories which make Afghanistan stand out as a case study in imbalanced ends, ways, and means: 1) strategic policy inconsistency divorced from the operational conditions in theater; 2) broken trust amongst and in the professional military forces in country, including both the of United States and its allied and partner nations, and; 3) the precedent this sets for employment of all-domain operations in the profession of arms in future war.

First, what were the contours of this policy inconsistency mentioned above? The paradigmatic Lykke model of strategic logic seeks to balance and even to harmonize a consistency of a nation's ends, ways, and means in national security policymaking in support of enduring strategic objectives. What are these three concepts and how do they relate? Lykke states,

> We can express this concept as an equation: strategy equals ends (objectives toward which one strives) plus ways (courses of action) plus means (instruments by which some end can be achieved). This general concept can be used as a basis for the formulation of any type strategy-military, political, economic and so forth, depending upon the element of national power employed.[4]

This model has become so synonymous with strategic national security policymaking that it has outgrown its original and solely military context. Indeed, it is paradigmatic across many U.S. federal agencies and even in international constituencies for defining how a nation can align and synchronize its geopolitical efforts.

This noted, ideally such national security policy ends should derive from or at least be nested under a reasoned and coherent grand strategy; in the case of the United States, this would be one that all political parties, governing institutions, and even citizens can agree upon as a correct geopolitical trajectory. The famous example for America is, of course, the Truman Administration's decision to counter the rise of Soviet-sponsored communism and socialism anywhere in the world in the wake of World War II. Subsequent presidential administrations, whether Republican or Democrat, agreed upon and upheld this as a grand strategy *sine qua non* for America until the fall of the Berlin Wall in 1989 and the dissolution of the Soviet Union in 1991. To that end, then, America consistently (for the most part) applied the application of its conceptual ways (the ideas which undergird policy achievement and become its operating mechanisms) and the purchase of its means (the tangible assets which enable the functioning of the means) in pursuit of this policy end. So, for Afghanistan, when I adjure that the United States suffered from a lack of clearly defined and consistently applied national security ends for our nation in that theater, this had a derivative effect on the consistent application of its ways and the purchase of its means towards that same end. Put another way, if a nation gets its ends misaligned, it misaligns the entire policymaking process.

In Afghanistan, perhaps no one summed this up better in reviewing the multi-nation and alliance-based effort than did then United Kingdom Lieutenant General David Richards (later Chief of the Defence Staff), when he said that since January 2002, "There was no coherent, long-term strategy...We were trying to get a single coherent, long-term approach—a proper strategy—but instead we got a lot of tactics."[5]

What had occurred in that specific month and year which General Richards cited? Recall that the United States invasion of Afghanistan occurred in October 2001, ostensibly to destroy the proto state of the Taliban in punishment for their role in abetting Osama bin Ladn and Al Qaeda for that terrorist organization's attack upon the United States on September 11, 2001. Moreover, this was the first historical instance of the North Atlantic Treaty Organization (NATO) invoking the core doctrine of mutual response enshrined in Article V of that treaty, which enjoins all nations to respond militarily if another member nation is attacked; NATO nation troops were quicky joining the fight. Yet just three months after that invasion and while the Taliban were decimated and in retreat, the United States changed its operational goal to shift away from the Taliban to pursuing Osama bin Ladn himself and destroying Al Qaeda as a network. Thus, the strategic mission changed by degrees to one of denying Al Qaeda a return to Afghanistan as a safe staging and training base to a global pursuit of the organization and its leader, a strategic end with a necessarily different application of both ways and means.[6]

This decision set the tone for the next twenty years of United States and NATO vagary about the strategic end to be achieved in Afghanistan. It was not significantly broached again as to a conclusion for America and its alliance partners until the first Biden Administration issued a new Presidential Policy Decision in March-April 2021, which was then debated and agreed upon at a NATO Ministers Special Meeting in August of that year. To be clear, both the Biden Administration and NATO had politically agreed upon concluding the military mission in Afghanistan; what had not been agreed upon was the plan for doing so. To our theme, the strategic end had now changed again; what had not been adjusted were the application of fresh ways and means to achieve that end. As Jamie Shea noted regarding the two decades worth of effort in support of the Afghan national government, military and police forces: "If the NATO troops left prematurely and the Taliban returned to power, these gains would be jeopardized."[7]

What were the accompanying conditions on the ground at this time? Basically, by mid-late summer 2021, President Biden had announced that the United States would leave Afghanistan completely by September 11, 2021, the twentieth anniversary of Al Qaeda's 9/11 attack on America. This pronouncement initiated a series of cascading events in-country, each iterative but mutually weakening of the next. First, the United States abandoned Bagram Airbase in early July, leaving a key strategic outpost in country (only 40 km north of the capital Kabul), solely in the hands of Afghan National Army (ANA) and Afghan National Police (ANP) forces. As Lyse Doucet wrote at the time, "Bagram is a bellwether of what's to come…(and) is vital—in symbolic and strategic ways. Taliban fighters, advancing in districts across the country, have this prize in their sights."[8] What this revealed was a second and related operational condition, and that was that the United States was not coordinating such moves with either the Afghan Federal Government or the ANA and ANP, and even its NATO alliance partner forces on the ground.

Indeed, the Afghan Federal Government felt abandoned and officials quickly began preparations to depart both them and their families out of country. Further, this deprived NATO forces of the planning, preparation, and execution for withdrawal, a complex military mission under the best of circumstances. This then emplaced Afghan, American, and NATO forces and civilian, contractor personnel and their families at immense tactical risk of attack by the advancing Taliban. Indeed and as all American efforts canalized into Kabul and the Hamid Karzai International Airport (HKIA), this left Afghan and even American civilians and their families left to their own initiative to both get to Kabul and then fight to enter HKIA in hopes of evacuation, but often at risk of familial separation and with no strategic plan in place for refugee transport, resettlement, or assimilation.

Once the suicide bombing occurred at Abbey Gate on 26 August, killing almost 200 people including Afghan civilians, 2 United Kingdom citizens, and 13 U.S. military personnel, the conditions for an only semi-organized abandonment of country by U.S. and NATO forces were set. This emplaced all left behind, including countless Afghan nationals who had supported the war effort, under threat of death, subject both to the dictates of the Taliban and its theocratic political ideology, its lack of ability to assume basic governing capacities, and its thirst for revenge.[9] In the later words of one young woman named Sammima—a former ANA veteran—"Thousands of girls like me are receiving threats, face an uncertain future and are being tracked by the Taliban…The U.S. and the international community said they would support us no matter what. But they have forgotten us."[10]

Why is a review of this painful case study necessary in order to better understand both moral and spiritual injury in war? Recall that we began this book with two controlling ideas: 1) these types of wounds are regnant in both individuals and communities, and;

2) that these types of wounds thus occur at not only the tactical but also the operational and strategic levels of war. The fall of Afghanistan in 2021 is a case study detailing both these truths.

If we draw on Jonathan Shay's concept of *themis* (the nature of a military force as a type of moral agent in itself), then we can discern that such a force exists on a "moral compact" of trust. Indeed, in the contemporary American profession of arms, the All-Volunteer Force rests on such an inchoate, powerful, trust-based bond between a warrior and his or her comrades, certainly, but also between a warrior and his or her American nation and people. However, today the distance between the strategic, operational and tactical levels of war is vastly reduced from previous conflicts, thus magnifying effects at one level almost instantaneously at another level (either positively or negatively).

This moral compact is a predicate of contemporary nation-state warfare, particularly borne out of the First and Second World Wars and the Cold War, collectively, and codified in modern alliance collective security treaties such as that governing the North Atlantic Treaty Organization (again for example, with NATO Article V covering mutual response and which governed initial alliance deployments in the wake of 9/11). At all levels, this is even codified in military law, policy, regulation and doctrine, for example in the concept today of "Interoperability" (human, procedural, and technical), where trust undergirds the forces of allied and partner nations. Thus, this moral compact of trust in contemporary war is both immediately horizontal and vertical, nowhere more so than at the global strategic level.

I believe that the United States' precipitous, ill-planned and uncoordinated withdrawal from Afghanistan in August 2021 broke the moral compact with her own and allied and partner nation warriors.[11] In doing so, this created an immense strategic trust barrier which the national will have to be overcome in successfully prosecuting future all-domain operations in future war. This cannot be overlooked or dismissed; trust remains endemic to victory.[12] As former National Security Advisor and U.S. Army Lieutenant General H. R. McMaster states:

> In America, the lack of commitment to win in war, apparent in a humiliating surrender to the Taliban and an ignominious retreat from Kabul, risks eroding trust between servicemen and women and their civilian and military leaders... American warriors won't long trust a society that doesn't believe in what the nation is fighting for—as they kill others and risk their own lives.[13]

Russo-Ukraine and Israel-Iran: Observations on the Nature and Character of War

The reasons we have reviewed Afghanistan as a case study in the ruptured social and martial trusts which undergirds war is that, at least for Americans, this event continues to shape our collective thinking about war. For America, this is our latest collective memory of how we as a nation initiated, prosecuted, and concluded a war; it shapes our thinking still. Yet what of the new conflicts in both the Russo-Ukraine and Israel-Iran wars? With American attitudes about Afghanistan as a baseline, how do its citizens now look at these two most recent conflicts, and what do they mean for our understanding about future war?

Regarding both Russo-Ukraine and Israel-Iran, and to be positively balanced, there do appear some hopeful tactical and operational developments on the battlefield, particularly in the Near East. First, Israel's destruction of Iran's air defense systems during an air attack in October 2024 has seriously degraded the latter nation's defensive capability and rendered it open to further attack while conversely reducing its military offensive capabilities. Linked to this is the destruction of the Hezbollah leadership in a pair of sequential cell phone and walkie-talkie attacks in September 2024, which though not having claimed responsibility, was further positively attributed to Israel's *Shin Beit* intelligence services. Next, Hezbollah then entered into agreement with Israel for a cease-fire in southern Lebanon, which in turn lead to a framework negotiation of a cease-fire with Hamas in the Gaza Strip. Then, and perhaps most cataclysmic of all, the Turkish-backed insurgent group Hayat Tahrir al-Sham on 7 December 2024 forced the abdication of the Bashar al-Assad Regime in Syria, effectively neutering an Iranian proxy—particularly logistically—that channeled resources to both Hezbollah and Hamas, as well as providing Russia with a strategically vital air and naval base from which to project power to the Mediterranean and beyond.[14] Little wonder, then, that many strategic observers have said that these sequential and interrelated operational developments on multiple battlefields have strategically weakened Iran as a regional hegemon and increased its domestic instability, due to its increasing economic isolation.[15]

The Russo-Ukraine War seems to have settled into a stalemate, though Ukraine temporarily held onto territorial gains made in its incursion into Kursk Oblast, even in facing additional but combat-inexperienced troops from the Democratic People's Republic of Korea.[16] Though uncertainty of the future remains, to particularly the holding of any ceasefire, negotiations now distinctly appear possible.

However, and to return to our work's central subject while sounding a hopeful yet cautious tone, by studying the internal individual and collective woundedness of moral and spiritual injury from war, particularly these wars in both Russo-Ukraine and Israel-Iran, it is possible to renew our understanding of the profession of arms. At its core, it is a values-based enterprise that, so controlled, can be regulated. Values, principles, and beliefs still drive the conduct of war. Based on my prior service as an Army chaplain with multiple operational and combat deployments, I am not naïve. I have seen first-hand war's destruction of men and women body and soul, of their families, of their communities, and sometimes of their nation-states, to include both combatants and noncombatants. I also have served long enough in the profession of arms to know that a war always does end, but also to ask: how is it initiated, why is it fought, and, most importantly, what are the political goals necessary to achieve in its conclusion? Although these questions may seem facile, it is amazing how often such questions drift from the awareness of parties in war, particularly at the strategic level; they demand constant focus, analysis, update, and ultimately, the application of political will in decision-making. Indeed, the moment is delicate. It is also difficult for any administration. Gideon Rose states:

> Ending the wars in Ukraine and Gaza are at the top of President Donald Trump's foreign policy agenda, and many expect the new administration to change American policy in both. It may well try to. But unless Russian President Vladimir Putin and Israeli Prime Minister Benjamin Netanyahu play along, Trump could easily find himself shifting back toward the Biden administration's approach in both theaters—because U.S. interests and geopolitical realities don't change with the election returns.[17]

In a more abbreviated format, then, and building upon the distinction between both the nature and the character of war, we offer some ethical reflections arising from both conflicts which mark either salient boundary crossings or boundary supports of "deeply held" communal experiences of moral and spiritual injury.

A. THE NATURE OF WAR and RUSSO-UKRAINE and ISRAEL-IRAN:

- Clausewitz's Observation Holds True—War remains an expression of broader political disagreements and decisions (or indecisions), though attenuated by historical ideologies, religious beliefs, failures of diplomacy, past grievances, greed, etc.[18] Essentially, neither of these two conflicts indicates that war is moving away from being existentially tied to political disputes or power struggles. This is true even though the Israel-Iran conflict was catalyzed by the 7 October 2023 attack of

Hamas—a terrorist organizations but an Iranian proxy acting at the tacit approval and logistical support of that nation-state—into Israel. Seeing these conflicts in this way removes some of the mystery or concern that war as a phenomenon is somehow changing in ways we do not understand…just the opposite. War is and will remain a contest of wills in which achieving political ends remain the ultimate prize, whether a combatant is a nation-state, sub-state actor, or people group. In point of fact, the brazen nature of how both Russia and Hamas (on behalf of its parent Iran) initiated these wars bears this out, as the world was shocked not only at the speed and ferocity of the initial assaults but how much they represented a naked grab for power by both belligerents through their stated enemy's destruction. If this remains an immutable principle of war, then nothing in either of these conflicts obviates that, and whether future war is fought at the nation-state level or below, relying on this truism can guide how and why such wars are fought.

- Geopolitical Values, Principles, and Beliefs are Paradigmatic—Even so, both these conflicts are reminders that people groups and nation-states will fight for a collectively non-negotiable or a demarcated social moral boundary worth upholding (individual combatants, less so). Thus, these conflicts do not mean that war is moving away from any type of concern around values, principles, and beliefs at a collective or communal level. Again, just the opposite. Although political disputes and power disagreements remain at the heart of war, such internal collective concerns around values remain just as operative as motivating forces to make *ad bellum* decisions to initiate conflict.
- National Will Remains Vital—However, sustaining war is another matter separate from initiating it. Here, perhaps, the limitations of values, principles, and beliefs as ongoing

motivations for continuing war are reached. Both these conflicts indicated that a nation-state or people groups' enduring motivation to fight, what we may broadly term national will, remain paradigmatic for seeing conflict through to termination. Both people groups and nation-states remain beholden to whatever the tides of collective will for war are (or are not) operative, as war is corrosive to a body politic and the sustained support of a people is limited. This may seem self-evident, but indeed both in the Russo-Ukraine and Israel-Iran wars indicate, war is not changing such that peoples or nation-states have an unceasing desire to fight on despite the costs.

- Strategic Preparedness is Difficult and is Limited, yet Necessary for Victory—This statement refers to a people group or nation state's total ability to *securely* raise, equip, train, deploy, employ, and redeploy a military force.[19] A critical component here is a nation successfully fusing its defense appropriation and acquisition requirements with industry, technology, healthcare, transportation, and especially economic nodes in coherent means to enact strategy and to achieve policy. No strategic combatant is immune from the more mundane considerations of whether it can achieve what American joint military doctrine terms "operational reach," a necessary global precondition to victory in an era of all-domain operations.[20]
- Grand Strategy is Paradigmatic—This presupposes, however, that people groups and nation-states have a comprehensive, guiding strategic vision for what they are trying to achieve that synchronizes all their instruments of national power (in coordination effectively with allies and partner nations) to mobilize and maintain national will.[21] No recent example of a nation's failure to maintain this alignment towards a conflict's strategic objective in support of grand strategy exceeds that

of the disastrous, precipitous American withdrawal from Afghanistan in August-September 2021.[22]

- To be historically balanced, though, we must see that it was the first Trump Administration's decision to conclude a peace accord with the Taliban that fuelled their military resurgence in theater. Also, by February 2021, the new Biden Administration publicly said that it was bound by that agreement and had no alternative but to carry it out. Here, the salient point is that the incoming presidential administration chose to accelerate the outgoing administration's decision to end the American campaign, against the later-publicly known military advice of its most senior military leaders. Therefore, the strategic conclusion of America's two-decade military campaign in the country was not a fait accompli which could not be paused or reversed. In this way, both administrations used the same tack: changing American national security policy aims for their own exigent political purposes. As per Craig Whitlock cited earlier in this chapter, this was precisely the problem across two decades beginning with both the Bush and Obama Administrations: American national security policy ends kept shifting but without any accompanying adjustment of ways and means to achieve them. America's exit from Afghanistan resulted, in large part, to its lack of a coherent grand strategy that synchronized its immediate national security and alliance efforts.

- While some may infer that I support one administration or another, I do not and remain apolitical. Rather, that for which I have equal disdain is the lack of strategic policy continuity across multiple presidential administrations. This leads to a derivative question amongst our warriors and their families, our allies and partner nation forces, and even our own people: is America strategically trustworthy in war—at its beginning, middle, and end? To not be so produces the strategic conditions for moral and spiritual injury that exist long after the guns of any battlefield fall silent. It is encouraging to note, in a perhaps counterintuitive way, that both the Russo-Ukraine and Israel-Iran wars continue to evidence this truism.

B. THE CHARACTER OF WAR and RUSSO-UKRAINE and ISRAEL-IRAN:

Continuing this more abbreviated format, then, let us offer some ethical reflections about how these conflicts are changing the character of war, and what this means for either boundary crossings or boundary supports of "deeply held" communal experiences of moral and spiritual injury (especially the former).

- Noncombatant Immunity is a Value Not to be Attacked but is Not Immutable—Russia, Hamas, Hezbollah, the Houthis in Yemen, and to a degree Israel, have deliberately targeted and attacked civilian population sets and the key societal infrastructures that support human security. In this way, civilians have been now cast as a "Center of Gravity" in war, capable of being both attacked and defended. Here, what was previously seen as a freshly enduring ethical stricture on war arising from the epochal conflicts of the 20th century is now potentially at risk of permanent dissolution. Moreover, this is not without societal costs upon the character of a people or nation-state, as Omer Bartov has so poignantly and accurately noted for both the Israel and its military forces.[23]
- Technology is Increasing Prudentialism in Targeting—Particularly both Ukraine and Israel are making extensive use of precision-targeting through satellites, drones, cellphones and walkie talkies, mass leaflet notifications, and then close air support to achieve greater tactical, operational, and even strategic effects in their use of direct and indirect fires. The

results have been staggeringly successful for both nation-states. For Ukraine and in the face of a seemingly indiscriminate mass targeting of its population centers and infrastructure by Russia, it has countered by selectively, accurately, and creatively targeting Russian forces and logistical nodes using self-made drones, satellite-linked special forces, and western-provided deep-strike missiles to foil Russian unit attacks and to interdict Russian lines of communications and supply.[24] For Israel, it has used counterintelligence-based targeting to disrupt Hezbollah command and control, coordinated air attack to destroy almost the entire Iranian air defense network, and of course mass leaflet drops to warn Gazan civilians of pending air and missile strikes. To the extent that such technology should or does reduce noncombatant risk, this could be seen as a good. However, and to almost universal opprobrium, Israel has come under fierce international condemnation and increasingly corroded its internal domestic national will by over-targeting civilian populations using such technological means.

- The Line between Semi-autonomous and Autonomous Weapons Systems is Blurring—Iran, Russia, and Hezbollah are especially using so-called "dumb" drones and rockets which, when launched, are released from human control but, when used in mass, can have increased probability of targeting effectiveness and lethality, particularly against civilian population centers. Such would be categorized as Lethal Autonomous Weapons Systems (LAWS), and which save for the human who has programmed their original computer software (if indeed so engineered), are "fire and forget" weapons designed to remove such systems from human control once launched against a target.[25] Moreover, by purchasing the design specifications and production rights from its ally Iran, Russia has now begun internal domestic production at scale of such weapons systems. This is increasingly advancing their lethality through Russian advancements in its computer software, aeronautical engineering, and increase of munitions payload on these platforms, resulting in a higher targeting effectiveness and lethality when employed against Ukrainian civilian targets.

- Alliances are Again Rearing Their Heads—Current, increasing geopolitical alliances center around politico-economic synchronization (such as in the EU, ASEAN, or the BRICS) and synchronization of military forces, weapons and munitions sharing, and leveraging fresh technologies at scale (such as in NATO, the BRICS, and AUKUS). However, as with Iran and Russia sharing drone technology and production rights, this is not all one-sided. For example, and since prior to Russia's invasion of Ukraine, Great Britain has been sharing signals, human, and satellite intelligence effectively and continually with Ukraine to give its military forces a competitive intelligence, surveillance, and reconnaissance competitive edge on the battlefield.[26] Yet also and more recently, the DPRK has been sending its troops to augment Russian forces in Kursk Oblast, but seemingly without a tangible battlefield advantage for Russia, except to relieve pressure on its forces.
- Collective Security Agreements are Under Strain from National Interests—An example of such an agreement formalized in an alliance treaty is found in NATO, which shares both a commitment to collective security for all alliance nations, formalized in its famed Article V guaranteeing mutual defense by all nations if one is attacked. However, during both these conflicts, what is becoming clear is that national interests are often supplanting such extra-national agreements, and this is particularly true relative to the manning, training, and equipping of military forces. For example, in 2022, German Chancellor Olaf Scholz famously

intoned before the *Bundestag* that Russia's invasion of Ukraine occasioned a fresh *Zeitenwende* in support of NATO and Ukraine, illustrated by his call for an immediate allocation of 100 Billion Euros for increasing German defense capability and an annual promise to achieve spending of 2% of GDP towards defense promised by all NATO members in the 2014 Wales Agreement.[27] Germany has failed to achieve either famed promise. However, other examples abound that such geopolitical agreements have their limits, most recently when Russia declined to aid Syrian President Bashar al-Assad at the request of Iran when the Assad regime was in peril from Hayat al-Tahrir forces. Indeed, this lends a sanguine perspective to such agreements and their utility in the face of real military threat; national interests and realities always predominate.

- All-Domain Operations are the Future of the Military Instrument of National Power—Finally, the character of war is demonstrating that, at least at the nation-state level, All-Domain Operations (ADO) will predominate in future strategic war. Such operations dictate that war will be waged simultaneously, continuously, and synchronically with allies and partner nations in the land, sea, air, cyber, and space domains of war, both in the homeland and abroad around the globe. Note, for instance, that this means for the first time in human history, a synthetic domain of war (Cyber) will fully integrate into a nation's strategic preparedness for conflict. Put another way and relative to the observation that strategic preparedness is paradigmatic for a nation's calculus towards victory, one reason that is so is that such defense capacity must be exercised through its total forces at sea, on land, in the air, in space, and in cyberspace. Moreover, this must be done in concert with allied and partner nation forces, occasioning a different set of problems around transnational secure communications and intelligence sharing, but particularly for NATO nations, these conditions seem to be being met. Moreover and on its own, Israel is fully employing ADO in every battlefield context, that has allowed it to achieve competitive advantage (if not victory) over Iran and its proxy forces in Gaza, Lebanon, Syria, and the Red Sea.

Of Values and Future War

If the statements above are some of the tangible strategic insights that can be drawn from these current conflicts, then these presage some larger questions that need to be examined socially in at least the American context; though it could be argued that they are relevant for most Western democracies and their professional military forces. Essentially, these are communal questions that Americans should be asking themselves about their values relative to their profession of arms, if indeed our military forces are to remain representative of and accountable to our client in the body politic.

First, we must ask whether we can regain trust (and perhaps trustworthiness) in the body politic. Such trust is, of course, both reflexive to and paradigmatic for the *profession* of arms, a point that numerous theorists have consistently made despite their differences on how those professions do or should function. Recent political history in the United States has shown that many people are losing faith rapidly that their national government is truly interested in and responsive to their personal needs and communal welfare. At the heart of this diminution of political faith is a corrosion of national trust, in our political leaders, processes, and efficient operations. There is, then, a growing and reflexive tide of pessimism and doubt in the efficacy of American democracy, but underlying this is a deeper crisis of trust in not only the structures that hold together American society but also in each other as fellow citizens who, regardless of political perspective, are all committed to the welfare of each other and to national success. Indeed, as Gerard Baker so aptly states:

> At the heart of America's political and cultural turmoil is a crisis of trust. In the space of a generation, the people's confidence in their leaders and their most important institutions to do the right thing has collapsed...As public faith in the performance, credibility and integrity of these institutions has collapsed, so too has mutual trust—the social glue that holds the country together. Americans have become suspicious of one another, distrusting their fellow citizens as much as they distrust foreign adversaries.[28]

Second, however, and coming from this, is whether the American people will relearn to trust their professional military forces, and allied to this, whether our martial colleagues amongst our allies and partner nations will do so as well.[29] The late Chief of Staff of the U.S. Army, General Raymond Odierno, succinctly and aptly stated that such trust is the "glue" that holds military units together, particularly amidst the ever-increasing tempo and moral ambiguity of war.[30] Indeed, this is precisely the point Jonathan Shay was raising when he talked of the communal threat to martial forces by unchecked moral injury in combat. Pursuant to the Afghanistan case study with which opened this chapter, then, I do not think it advisable or tenable for the American profession of arms to continue presuming that its client, the American people, will always imbue their military forces with such trust.

Although the primary takeaway of that debacle could be assigned as a political failing of the Biden Administration, it cannot but have contributed to the downward trend in social respect for and trust in the American profession of arms. This is a trend which a new or subsequent presidential administration cannot by itself reverse; such trust will have to be re-earned by the profession of arms amongst our people. As well, such trust will have to be re-earned by the American military forces which will predominate in the future joint force amongst allied and partner nation colleagues, who cannot be blamed for wondering as to American political resolve to finish the fights in which we ask them to join us.

Third, the United States (or any nation) must as a nation have a clear discussion about which national values are worth fighting and dying for. Warriors and their families must continuously ask themselves this question. In recent years, this has been attenuated with particularity depending upon the conflict in which one was being deployed. Indeed, we aspire to have a reflective and reasoning military force in which professionals have the moral sensitivity and nuanced thinking to make such assessments. To have a force less than this with the latent power of destruction which we wield would be disastrous. However, such moral sensitivity and nuanced thinking must also be regnant within our client, the American people, as in all people groups and nation-states.

Ours is not such an out-sourced profession of arms that our people abdicate the responsibility to decide what values will govern our nation's use of military force, either now or in the future. If understanding moral and spiritual injury can aid us in answering this question both individually and collectively, then this process now will serve us in larger ways in the future. To borrow a pastoral truism which also governs ethics in the profession of arms: If we as a nation cannot decide for what we are willing to send our sons and daughters to risk injury and die in war, then we will never truly know that by which we truly wish to live.

Finally, a related question of values must surely guide whether people groups and nation-states will even retain their professions of arms (and thus such professionals) in the face of technological pressures to abdicate human responsibility for the prosecution of war. Samuel Huntington, of course, famously intoned that "the management of violence" was the province of the military professional on behalf of its social client, a proposition with no small degree of implied risk in the era of thermo-nuclear war in which made such an assertion.

Nonetheless and in conjunction with Marshall's assertion that the "soul of the soldier is everything" relative to victory in war compared to technology, then it seems an apropos social moment to renew these compacts of the profession arms. Indeed, as Clausewitz advocated, this is a needed requirement for not only victory but also social survival and *post-bellum* peace, a type of agreement of what's at stake in war.[31] Technology, and especially the mushrooming power of artificial intelligence, cannot decide such a question for us and cannot allow us to abdicate our responsibility to do so. At the heart of the major social questions about war which must be re-examined today, none is more important than the decision about the nature of war and that it can and must remain a regrettable but necessarily human enterprise.

So why is an exploration of values in war necessary to explore moral and spiritual injury? Or, we might reverse the question and ask: Why is the study of moral and spiritual injury helpful to reflecting on the role of values in war, particularly in an era of professionalized militaries? In part, it is that by attending with specificity to the nature of moral and spiritual injury in war, we are necessarily and rightly led to examine the wider issue of values and war.

The current conflicts which we've examined in this chapter—the chaotic nature of the American withdrawal from Afghanistan and the current wars taking place in the Russo-Ukraine and Israel-Iran contexts—are forcing societies to examine the nature and character of war again, particularly relative to the values, principles, and beliefs which must undergird it. If for no other reason than a prudential calculation of cost-benefit analysis, for example, a small but ever-coalescing group of thought is emerging in moral and spiritual injury studies to examine prevention of the malady rather than reaction to it.

I concur with ethicists Marc LiVecche, Nathan White, and others who believe that moral and spiritual injury can be, if not prevented, at least ameliorated in their deleterious effects on the individual through intentional reflection, training, self-awareness, and decision-making.[32] However, I further think that this can and should be also true at the collective level of war—so for units, forces, and nation-states—but that the process is the same: reflection, training, self-awareness, and decision-making. For both a person and a force, this process leads to clarity in deliberately and consonantly acting in the crucible of conflict in accord with our underlying values, principles, and beliefs. Understanding how current conflicts are shaping the nature and character of war help us here, but in the end, we still must ask and answer the question: "What do I, or we, believe?" Only by doing so can we hope to make any decision about when, how, for what reason we will fight in war—there is no shortcut to this ethical decision.

Strategic Moral and Spiritual Injury

It is helpful, perhaps necessary, to conclude this chapter with a word regarding why I believe that both the Russo-Ukraine and Israel-Iran wars embody strategic moral and spiritual injury. Recall that two of the core ideas of this book are that: moral and spiritual injury are not only tactical but also strategic problems in war, and quickly becoming "wicked problems" for planning in future war, and; that moral injury particularly is not only a phenomenon based in emotional discordance but also ethical disequilibrium, and again, this is true for individuals as well as communal groups, even people groups and nation-states. The two conflicts listed above clearly illustrate these ideas. How so?

First, though both the Russo-Ukraine and Israel-Iran wars are demonstrating that the nature of war is largely static while the character of war is changing, both categories further illustrate that at the strategic level of war, the former category remains a type of hedge against moral and spiritual injury, while the latter category opens seams and gaps for these maladies to occur. If these conflicts demonstrate that values, principles, and beliefs remain paradigmatic to war, then this becomes something around which nation-states and professional militaries can plan, prepare, execute, and then assess in war. If these conflicts indeed show that values, principles, and beliefs remain an enduring truth amidst these new nation-state conflicts, then this can become a type of strategic protective factor which will prevent moral and spiritual injury in future war.

Nation-states and their militaries can indeed intentionally invest both their human, fiscal, and intellectual capital in increasing the teaching and inculcation of values, principles, and beliefs in both their military forces—particularly in leader development—and in their civilian populations. Essentially, ethical instruction and pedagogy as factors in human development need not be relegated only to the professional militaries which are too often outsourced the defense of the modern nation-state. Rather, such ethical instruction and pedagogy in national values, principles, and beliefs can and should become a paramount effort in civil preparedness for war. In this way, both military forces and the peoples they serve can better be strategically prepared for war, including both the experience of and recovery from moral and spiritual injury.

However, this is only one potential application relative to future war. If the other observations on the unchanging nature of war in both these conflicts (e.g. that Clausewitz's truism of war being an extension of politics by other means, that national will remains paramount, that strategic preparedness is both difficult but evermore necessary as a precondition for victory, and that grand strategy is paradigmatic), then again, these taken with ethical instruction in national values, principles, and beliefs can collectively become a basis for nation-states successfully preparing for future war. Moreover, these can become protective factors in those nation-states ameliorating the efforts of strategic moral and spiritual injury in both their professional military forces and their peoples.

Second, however, is a cautionary note. If the observations about the nature of war from the Russo-Ukraine and Israel-Iran conflicts demonstrate that some things are immutable about war as a phenomenon, then my further observations about the changing character of war from these same conflicts demonstrate that these will provide openings for moral and spiritual injury to occur across nation-states, their militaries, and the peoples they serve. For instance, both these wars clearly show that the international value and norm of noncombatant immunity is not only under direct threat but also is now being used as a tactic in which military forces have, can, and will attack to achieve a competitive advantage in war.

As will be seen in the next chapter, gone for now is the ideal that civilians should remain protected from direct attack, targeting, and exploitation in war. Instead, both these current wars demonstrate that even the regrettable notion of "collateral damage" amongst civilian noncombatants who are inadvertently caught up in the chaos of combat is gone. Rather, military forces of all stripes are indicating that attacking, displacing, wounding, and killing of such noncombatant civilians is an ethically acceptable and tactically advantageous aim in war. This further means that large population concentrations of such peoples—particularly in the densely-populated urban environs, which will increasingly be the context for future war—will almost surely be intentionally and grievously attacked with the rapaciously-growing weapons systems and munitions regnant in future war.

Unless nation-states determine and enshrine the protection of such noncombatants in future war, and make the necessary tactical, operational, and strategic decisions to uphold such a vital strategic ethical principle, the very populations and people groups which military forces are seeking to advantage through war will inadvertently but increasingly be at risk for annihilation in future war. Even if majorities of population centers survive future war, the employment of this tactic produces a clear and compelling case that moral and spiritual injury will strategically embed themselves as outcomes of war which will last long after the destruction of the battlefield has ceased.

The observations offered about these conflicts detailing disturbing changes to the character of war offer further seams or gaps through which future moral and spiritual injury will, almost certainly, occur in future war. Along with targetable noncombatant immunity, then, we may see: technology's increasing prudentialism in targeting; the evolutionary blurring of distinctions between semi-autonomous and autonomous weapons systems; the increasing challenges and opportunities presented by strengthening alliances; the fact that collective security agreements are under strain if not rupture, and; that all-domain operations will dominate nation-states' use of the military instrument of national power. Taken either in part or in whole, while some of these may and do appear as desired outcomes of the changing character of war arising from the Russo-Ukraine and Israel-Iran conflicts, each can and likely will be used as by some future combatants as seams or gaps to attack to achieve a competitive advantage in future war.

For example, if alliances rupture and collective security falls under strain or dissolves completely, individual nation-states may increasingly resort to the maximalization of semi-autonomous and autonomous weapons systems with their increasing fidelity in targeting to repeatedly and with greater effect attack the noncombatant population centers which will be the arena for future war. At the speed and scale of future war with potential combatants such as the United States and the Peoples Republic of China, the resulting death and destruction will dwarf both the present Russo-Ukraine and Israel-Iran wars. Moreover, it will make the concomitant increase in strategic and moral injury in any *jus post bellum* recovery from war a problem set of almost incalculable estimation.

Nonetheless, the harbingers of these trends of future war are on ample display now. We need not be surprised if and when they arise. Rather and in a hopeful vein, they can at least be strategically ameliorated if nation-states and the professional militaries incorporate them today into their planning, preparation, execution, and assessments for such conflicts. In this way, strategic moral and spiritual injury in war can at least be blunted, if not prevented, and perhaps even serve a greater *telos* of any war, the re-establishment of a more just and lasting peace.

4

BOUNDARY MAINTENANCE: FUTURE WAR

Upholding the Bulwark of the Just War Tradition

What are the moral and ethical boundaries which we must retain if societies are to achieve peace after war in the future? Framed in my taxonomy, what are the values, principles, and beliefs which will be necessary to maintain war as a human enterprise that aligns it with social norms and needs, able still to achieve even a relative measure of peace and maintenance of the common good despite its attendant destruction?

Some might consider that war has crossed a technological divide in which this is impossible, but many, including the author, would disagree. The present strategic context bears resemblance to that of the mid-1950s, where the threat of thermonuclear war seemed to obviate the need for ethics to regulate the profession of arms, as humanity's destruction appeared a foregone conclusion. However, significant theological ethicists—particularly from Protestant and Roman Catholic Christianity—pushed back against such pessimism and reasserted the primacy of the Just War Tradition (JWT) as a regulating paradigm over even nuclear war.

However, as the world now lies firmly in the grip of great power competition and nation-state war—particularly in non-western contexts—it can rightly be asked whether the JWT has any fresh applicability to such a fractured geopolitical context, far different than the bipolarity of the Cold War. Indeed it does have applicability, particularly in the regulating capacity of *jus ad bellum* criteria to strategically assist nation-states in their decisions about when, where, why to initiate war, and certainly in *jus in bello* considerations about how to do so justly.

Rather than these criteria being the exception, as the character of war has moved from an early-21st century focus on counterinsurgency to large scale combat operations and in future to fully synchronized and simultaneous all-domain operations, prudential considerations will increasingly dominate nation-states and their considerations about conflict. The JWT can remain a bulwark for the regulation of war, but only as much as nation-states will so employ it, particularly in properly aligning ends, ways, and means in support of an elucidated grand strategy.

This is not to presume that there is a common framework for understanding the JWT. What the tradition entails differs slightly among proponents. From my perspective, the tradition (and it is not a theory) arises from a historical process of reasoning, debate, and writing about war and society going back at least two thousand years in principally Western nations. Thus, today I hold the JWT as entailing the following seven elements:

- Just Cause—war must be grounded in a morally just *causus belli* prior to conflict initiation.
- Right Authority—war must be sanctioned only by legitimate public authorities (for instance in democratic polities, the elected national representatives of a nation-state).
- Public Declaration—war should be subsequent to the above and declared openly prior to conflict initiation.
- Right Intent—war should seek to achieve a right or just end that governs it's *in bello* conduct.

- Proportional Means—war must be further governed *in bello* by employment of proportional military means commensurate with those used by each combatant.

- Last Resort—war should be initiated only when all other national instruments of power, particularly diplomacy, have failed to resolve competing political disputes.

- Reasonable Hope of Success—prior to initiation, a nation-state's political authorities must only assess that initiation of war contains a reasonable hope of achieving the unresolved aggrievements which underlie it.[1]

Additionally, we may note that arising from the cataclysmic wars of the twentieth century, the tradition is now understood as further encompassing four contemporary criteria:

- Noncombatant Immunity—military forces and individual armed combatants must refrain from the deliberate targeting of civilian noncombatants.

- Use of Minimum Force Necessary—similar to proportional means, war should be governed by a force-allocation level to only compel an enemy to cease hostilities (rather than utter and total destruction).

- Ethical Treatment of Enemy Prisoners of War and Detained Persons—under particularly the Geneva Conventions of 1947, combatant POWs and detainees are to be no longer seen as armed combatants but afforded humane care during their incarceration.

- Prohibition Against Inhumane Means or Tactics (*malum in se*)—finally, and particularly as technology increases the lethality of targeting, in war no means should be employed *in*

> *bello* which outside of war would reasonably be considered to be inhumane in their effects.[2]

The JWT remains a broad moral framework for thinking about how to initiate, prosecute, and even recover from war, as broadly flexible today as at any time. To be sure, the tradition has its limitations, not the least of which is that is often seen as inherently Western in its value-orientation (even to the point of risking bias in conceptualizing war), that it is seen as overly supportive of maintaining the primacy of the post-Westphalian nation-state system (as opposed to say being applicable to the ideologies of sub-nation-state forces or the cultural norms of either non-Western or non-nation-state people groups), and that it places too much of a regulating emphasis on ethics in war when the latter is more properly seen as an element of *realpolitik* in a world governed by hard power.

It is precisely this latter point that will continue to make the JWT applicable to a world in which the nature of war is principally unchanged, while the character of war is rapidly reshaping in critical ways.[3] Nonetheless, such a moral framework for thinking about war can seem woefully out of date, if not anachronistic, given our prior assessment about how the conflicts in both Russo-Ukraine and Israel-Iran have unfolded, a point needing acknowledgement. Indeed, as we shall see in the next section, these conflicts some to have eviscerated at least one of the major components of the contemporary JWT.

To be sure, employing the JWT is an exercise in judgment-making, or put alternatively, creating a moral framework about war. As Marc LiVecche has stated: "The just war tradition, presupposing a universal moral order that is, in limited ways, knowable, requires, necessarily so, the making of such judgments."[4] Indeed, we cannot escape applying such epistemological judgment-making about war, but fortunately, the JWT allows us a workable, if not imperfect, method for doing so.

Protecting Key Civilian Populations

The above admonition for an upholding of the JWT, however, as a moral framework for war raises a vital question: In both the current Russo-Ukraine and Israel-Iran wars, one critical ethical problem has been how (for both combatants and more broadly the international community) to respond to the deliberate attacking of key civilian population groups as a battlefield tactic? Indeed, of all the eleven historic and modern elements of the JWT listed above, the one which stands out most as under threat is that of noncombatant immunity. Any observer of both these conflicts might, simply by taking them as representative of all war (though as we have seen, they are not), wonder whether such an ethical parameter of noncombatant immunity is even worth upholding in future moral and ethical leadership in war for any combatant force.

This requires a survey of four particular ways in which this ethical parameter alone has been specifically threatened with extinction in these two conflicts. Such a survey cannot do justice here to the immense suffering which the following populations have endured, but it can at least raise again our awareness to their plight and a recommitment to their justice. Indeed, Vickie Barnette has stated: "The importance of attending to the needs of civilians, displaced persons, and POWs is not morally ambiguous in the way that other wartime decisions may be."[5] Just so and under the best of circumstance but, as we shall see, this is now directly under threat.

First, is the catalogued Russian war crime of slaughtering over 400 civilian noncombatants in and around the town of Bucha, UK and other municipalities from 24 February through 6 April 2022. Recall that on the former date, Russia's invasion plan called for an airborne operation to seize Kyiv's main airport followed by a type of double envelopment of armored forces from the north and east of the country, with the aim of decapitating Ukraine's federal government and quickly installing a Russian puppet regime.

Ukrainian forces brilliantly and courageously foiled the Russian airborne operation (and denied Russia air superiority for a time), penned up their adversary's northern advance along a single axis of attack (and subsequently defeated that entire force) and blunted the Russian advance coming from the eastern, Russian-occupied regions of Luhansk and Donetsk. When this occurred, it forced Russian commanders with a choice of either pressing the attack or retreating along their rear lines of communication, which they chose to do. However, in and around the town of Bucha (and other towns), garrisoned and then retreating Russian forces killed noncombatant civilians who posed no tactical threat as combatants. Indeed, as the Head of the U.N. Human Rights Monitoring Mission in Ukraine, Mathilde Bogner, stated in commenting on the U.N. investigative efforts:

> There are strong indications that the summary executions documented in this report may constitute the war crime of willful killing... Russian soldiers brought civilians to makeshift places of detention and then executed them in captivity. Many of the victims' bodies were found with their hands tied behind their backs and gunshot wounds to their heads.[6]

Russia's Foreign Ministry attempted to reverse blame for the killings. Then-spokeswoman Maria Zakharova stated, "Who are the masters of provocation? Of course the United States and NATO... In this case, it seems to me that the fact that these statements (about Russia) were made in the first minutes after these materials appeared leaves no doubt as to who 'ordered' this story."[7] Nonetheless, it is for these crimes (and others) that the International Criminal Court (ICC) in the Hague has issued arrest warrants for Russian President Vladimir Putin, former Minister of Defense Sergei Shoigu, and Chief of the General Staff Valery Gerasimov.[8] However, the ICC's investigations into Russian targeted killings of civilian noncombatants in Ukraine remains ongoing, both for evidence-gathering and for building prosecutorial case files against these leaders and other individual Russian soldiers.

This leads to a second example of how the targeting of noncombatants has been savagely seen in these wars, namely both through child kidnapping and hostage taking in general. As to the former war crime, Russia also made this an early tactic in the war but conducted this at scale, and according to investigators from the Organization for Security Cooperation in Europe (mirroring Ukrainian Government recorded claims by family members), since Russia's annexation of Crimea in 2014, over 20,000 Ukrainian children have been forcibly kidnapped and deported against their and their family's will to Russia, often undergoing "re-education" to nationalize them into Russian language, culture, history, customs, and religion.[9] Indeed, to date no more than several hundred children have been returned to their families back in Ukraine, though prior to Russia's main invasion in February of 2022, Ukraine had one of the highest institutionalization rates for children and teens in all of Europe, a situation which Moscow exploited to its advantage.[10] Additionally, this has led to the ICC to further issue an arrest warrant for Maria Alekseyevna Lvova-Belova, Commissioner for Children's Rights in the Office of the President of the Russian Federation, "...for the war crime of unlawful deportation of population (children) and that of unlawful transfer of population (children) from occupied areas of Ukraine to the Russian Federation."[11]

However, and we must wonder, whether this in part or in whole catalyzed the tactic of Hamas kidnapping Israeli civilians pursuant to its border incursion and killing spree of over 1,400 people on 7 October 2023? Certainly, for whatever reason, Hamas deliberately incorporated this tactic as a means to forestall any massive and immediate Israeli military response, going so far as to ferry their hostages—men, women, children, and the aged and infirm—into their underground tunnel networks throughout the territory of Gaza. The capturing of these 220 hostages, however, was nationally-agnostic, as there were a majority of Israeli citizens but those held included

Argentinian, German, French, Russian, American, Filipino, Thai, and Chinese citizens, from an aggregate of 25 nations.[12] Indeed, even now as a tenuous phased cease-fire between Israel and Hamas has held and Hamas uses each release as a spectacle to drive information operations (portraying their purported tactical power), there remain over 80 hostages who have not been released, and whom Hamas retains while demanding that Israel completely cease offensive operations and fully withdraw from Gaza, demands to which Israel refuses to comply.[13] Clearly, the taking and holding of hostages of any age is now seen by at least Russia and Hamas as tactically advantageous, if not strategically beneficial, despite the potential costs.

This noted, there is another aspect of particularly the Russo-Ukraine war that can be seen as a derivative outcome (if not a deliberately Russian-targeted effect) of combat, and that is the more than 7 million Ukrainians who have dispersed across not only Europe but also the world as part of a larger resettlement of refugees from the fighting. Many in the aftermath of the initial invasion turned westward and crossed national borders into either Poland, Slovakia, Hungary, or Romania. Many millions of others dispersed farther afield, including to Germany, France, Italy, the United Kingdom, and the United States.

What this has meant for Ukraine, of course, is that as the war has dragged on, these Ukrainians have ostensibly settled into a semi-permanent if not permanent state in these other countries. This has deprived Ukraine proper with some degree of manpower for its military forces, but certainly has deprived the nation of the human and intellectual capital necessary for its economy and services industries which are vital to the overall war effort. Moreover, it has created a social divide between those who left Ukraine and those who remained, such that now many of those who stayed and endured the fighting are voicing anger and desires for recrimination against their fellow citizens who decamped to foreign lands. As well, for the nations which did receive those Ukrainian refugees, particularly Poland (where over 2 million refugees resettled), their resettlement has proven no small undertaking, incurring fiscal, social, educational, health care, and economic costs unforeseen at the outset of the conflict.

While this movement cannot be seen in tandem with other refugee movements in and across Europe from prior wars of the early 21st century (for example from Afghanistan, Iraq, the African Sahel, or Syria, to name but a few), there is no question that this has become a major outgrowth of this particular war, one which Russia likely intended to achieve as a result of its initial invasion. How this situation will resolve after the fighting ceases will be a social challenge for Ukraine as it seeks to rebuild its fractured nation, and one which will be played out in locally in heart-rending detail amongst towns, villages, religious communities, and family systems.

A final aspect in which these wars have directly threatened noncombatant civilian populations is through the targeting of people by either religious or ethnic identity. Both the Russo-Ukraine and Israel-Iran wars bear frightening correlation to the afore-mentioned ethnic cleansing genocides in both Rwanda in 1994 and Bosnia-Herzegovina in 1995, where the world was seemingly awakened in the modern age to attempts to exterminate whole people groups based solely on their religious and/or ethnic heritage, though this tactic is, in fact, quite ancient in nature.

The late-twentieth and early twenty-first centuries have reminded ostensibly post-modern societies that the world has not evolved past the potential for such animosities and hatreds to fuel violence, persecution, and the deliberate targeting of people groups in war. Indeed, Russia's predicate for its invasion of Ukraine in 2022 was none other than its viewing of Ukraine as a non-nation-state, Ukrainians as a non-distinct sub-people under the "Kyivan Rus'" mythological construct, and itself and the Moscow Patriarchate as the historic religious descendent of all Slavic Orthodoxy dating back to the baptism of Volodymyr the Great in the Dnieper River outside Kyiv in the year 988.

As detailed earlier, in the Israel-Iran war, Hamas as a combatant willfully and deliberately targeted civilians, of course, in its assault on 7 October 2023. However, what the world was more shocked to see was their exploitation of social media in information operations in live-streaming and/or recording their atrocities—including rape, murder, desecration of corpses, and kidnapping—as both a propaganda and motivational tool for other potential jihadists around the globe. Shown to the world in real-time was Hamas's and its militants undisguised hatred of Jews and Judaism, notwithstanding that, as mentioned, many other nationalities were also killed, maimed, and kidnapped on that day. While both Hamas and its Iranian overlords claimed a mantel of simply rebelling against historic injustices perpetrated against the Palestinian peoples, Hamas's displayed barbarism undercut any semblance of credibility towards this claim; this was deliberate, brutalized warfare against Jews because they were Jewish, nothing more. Thus, both these conflicts seem to bear out, in grim detail, that both present and future conflicts are or can be fueled by a socialized pathological hatred of "the other" at the scale and speed of modern war. Rather than contemporary cultures having grown past such catalysts for war, future war will no doubt retain if not amplify them even beyond these current conflicts.

A summary of this review, then, places before us the undeniable ethical tension which future war will present: there will remain an ever-present balance between both advancing human security whilst correspondingly achieving national security in war. While this tension is not new to war, both the Russo-Ukraine and Israel-Iran wars present us with this tension but brought into sharper focus by the speed and scale of these wars. Moreover, with the deliberate targeting of noncombatant immunity in these wars—via killing, torture, rape, kidnapping, and hostage-taking—as a tactic in war, this only accentuates how balancing these two ethical tensions in future war will become more important in future wars, not less.

Practically, this means that particularly in terms of developing future national security leaders, maintaining the ethical balance between upholding both human and national security must move from being an implied to a specified task at the tactical, operational, and strategic levels of war…there is no getting around this requirement. As Tony Pfaff summarizes (using the taxonomy of theory):

> Just war treats sovereignty as a limit on action; human security sees it as a responsibility that motivates action. Just war theory emphasizes reaction; human security emphasizes prevention. Just war theory limits harm; human security promotes the good, not just for people within one's borders, but anywhere populations are threatened.[14]

In practical terms, this means that particularly at the strategic level of war, forcing a choice between either national security or human security is forcing a false dichotomy, for it is not an "either/or" but an "both/and" solution set. Moreover, it's not that nation-states will not make decisions based on their national interests; as we aver, they will. However, those interests need not be at the expense of human security interests as well. This means that it will require such national security leaders, whether uniformed or civilian, to lead with the moral courage in the decision-making process to uphold both requirements in pursuit of peace, justice, and the common good. Only in doing so can such leaders mitigate against the strategic moral and spiritual injury which, as we have tragically seen, leads to violating noncombatant immunity both during and after war.

Paying the Opportunity Costs of Restoration and Reconciliation

Economists have introduced into the common vocabulary a concept that bears on our discussion here, and that is the term "opportunity cost." Used frequently today, it is worth lingering over a definition: such costs are defined as "A benefit, profit, or value of something that must be given up to acquire or achieve something else. Because every resource (land, money, time, etc.) can be put to alternative uses, every action, choice, or decision has an associated opportunity cost. Opportunity costs are fundamental costs in economics, and are used in computing cost benefit analysis of a project. Such costs, however, are not recorded in the account books but are recognized in decision making by computing the cash outlays and their resulting profit or loss."[15]

This economic definition expressed in transactional monetary categories also corresponds to our consideration of strategic moral and spiritual injury. How so? Indeed, we may quickly intuit that such opportunity costs in war are the human capital of a nation's sons and daughters which it sends to war on its behalf. While persons are not a "zero sum game," to be sure, they are finite resources necessary to corporate human flourishing on many levels of human society. In essence and to correlate the above definition to this strategic moral and spiritual injury, warriors and their families are resources who "can be put to alternative uses" and if the nation chooses to expend those resources in combat and afterwards in enduring moral and spiritual injury, then such lost resources are not only tragic after-effects of war but also opportunity costs which the nation may, or may not have, adequately counted prior to the decision to initiate hostilities.

Yet there is a second corrosive opportunity cost of moral and spiritual injury to any nation, particularly within the force itself. First, in a profession of arms as described above (so a technically and tactically proficient force so discreet in its function that it lacks a corollary in the nation it serves), then moral and spiritual injury can radically demoralize the force preparing for future war. What is alluded to here is that if such wounded warriors remain in the ranks as the force so needs them to do by nature of its ongoing commitments to the fight, then their presence can either produce exemplars of resilience or degradation but not both. As a result, with a force such as America's current military—where the stigmatism of either perceived personal weakness or threats to career advancement often inhibit warriors from seeking care in the first place—both moral and spiritual injury can be subsumed under the veneer of unit readiness and ironically degrade such readiness over time. Thus, this often produces a derivative set of challenges:

1. There is the leadership challenge in maintaining motivation of and discipline amongst a formation where moral and spiritual injury is present, even amongst a small segment of that formation.

2. There is the tactical risk to that force that untreated moral and spiritual injury can lay the groundwork for the commission of future war crimes in future operations.

3. As mentioned previously in such a professionalized force, there is the strategic risk that at either general or flag officers exhibit ethical leadership failures arising from their own untreated moral and spiritual injury, when such failures corrode morale both within and without the force.

4. There is the regnant risk on the profession of it becoming an unreflective institution, in which in a leader's professional judgment values are not measured against political aims and military objectives to produce a feasible, suitable, and acceptable course of action.[16] In short, institutional values can become de-linked from plans, training and operations and, as a result, sidelined from incorporation into a command's organizational thinking, culture, and efficacy of military advice about the same to civilian political leaders.

5. Finally, there is the risk at every level of the force to its undergirding and critical family systems resulting from a loss of morale, trust, or belief in the profession of arms (and by

derivation, their correlation of that loss of trust to that family system's uniformed warrior commitment to the profession).

These are but some of the ways in which untreated moral and spiritual injury result in an opportunity cost to the profession of arms.

Recall that in modern conceptions of such a profession (particularly in the American context), this is a highly trained and technically and tactically proficient set of experts whom societies imbue with the mission of maintaining national security; the conscript force is dead. As a result, the need to maintain every protection of that force against such latent threats as moral and spiritual injury must be an opportunity cost saved against the above (and other) risks to such a socially vital profession. Harkening back to the opening of this chapter, this points to why such forces desperately and consistently need *more and not less* dedicated, curated time in moral and ethical leader development. In the press of any rush to outsource national security to either emerging technologies, weapons systems, or platforms, what cannot be abrogated is the profession's maintenance and even augmentation of its program of instruction towards moral and ethical leadership, Surely, such must be seen as a necessary investment against paying the opportunity cost of preventable moral and spiritual injury in the profession of arms.

However, this points to a larger consideration of the opportunity cost of moral and spiritual injury even beyond that profession, namely the threat to, as I've termed it, the pervasive and persistent nature of these injuries across a series of communal relationships. Here, I do not view the effects of these injuries as being confined to the warrior alone; by no means. Indeed, and as previously suggested in this book, these injuries are polyvalent in nature, such that a rupture within the mind and/or soul of the warrior always radiates outward from her or him, resulting in a series of concentric relationship ruptures with and to that warrior's family system, community, nation, and even God. This is what makes these injuries such a socially impactful and debilitating experience, but one which is never confined to the profession of arms alone. Rather, and as almost every nation recently or now engaged in war attests to, long after the physical wounds from the battlefield have healed, the moral and spiritual injuries resulting from war continue to linger and fester in ways that, if left untreated, leave permanent damage to the social fabric of that nation.

This is not to say that all such injuries can always and everywhere be avoided. In one way, this is part of the opportunity cost of war as a human phenomenon. However, what it is to say is that such a cost must be considered with forethought, assessed with specificity, and incorporated with intentionality into the national security decision-making process *prior* to war.

In modern, free nation-states, effective governance certainly enjoins on its national security professionals a costing of potential moral and spiritual injury to not only its military forces but also to its entire population. No nation-state can avoid paying all such costs, but neither should the awareness of such an opportunity cost be a surprising, mournful result of post-conflict "looking back" at how the populace decided to go to war, and then perhaps questioning whether the collective social decision to go to war was originally justified, and in my estimation according to the helpful criteria of the JWT. Considered modern governance requires that such state apparatuses as serve their peoples level with them before going to war about the costs that war will impose on the entire nation-state after war ceases.

Recovering the Sacred in War: Valuing Warriors, Families, and Citizens

Finally, and to conclude this book, I want to sound a hope-filled note about how societies might best prevent and recover from strategic moral and spiritual injury in future war, and that is to recover a sacred valuation of our warriors, families, and indeed all citizens. This surely exceeds the almost trite phraseology so common in American culture today, where a civilian happens to meet a serving or veteran service member and casually says "Thank you for your service." No, most of us who have been to war recognize that this phrase, though well-intentioned and offered perhaps in the uncomfortable silence where a civilian doesn't know how best to engage one who has gone to war on their behalf, ultimately lacks both meaning and conviction, despite its wide-spread societal usage. There must be another way.

Here, and returning to my own theological background and training, I want to advocate that nation-states and their military forces recover a sacred valuation of their individual warriors, families, and indeed all citizens. As previously mentioned in this book, I have long been concerned that the contemporary profession of arms has reduced assessing the worth of its warriors almost based solely on a prudential consideration of what they might do as a member of the force.

As technology increasingly demands that we assess its utility based on how it does or does not increase lethality on the battlefield and even victory in war, we cannot allow that mental model to inchoately dominate how we assess the men and women of our forces. Our people are worth more...eternally more...than what they do or don't do, as noble, worthy, and necessary are such tasks in defense of the republic.

We cannot reduce our estimation of such warriors, family members, and even citizens to only a consequentialist rendering of their utility. Rather, people are of inherent eternal worth simply by virtue of their existence, for each bears within themselves the *imago Dei* in and through which they were created, and in an through which they might hope to be eternally redeemed. Placing such a high value on the temporal and eternal worth of every person maintains our social moral and ethical sensitivity and derivatively raises the bar on any decision by a nation-state to go to war. Towards the central idea of this book, this further imbues each person with a renewed self-estimation that further posits that, even should they experience moral and spiritual injury in war, such is not permanent, and even that can be redemptive in restoring all relationships ruptured by war.

ENDNOTES

Preface

1 Reinhold Niebuhr, of course, was the pre-eminent Christian Realist of the 20th century, but located the roots of his theo-political outlook in the thinking St. Augustine, Bishop of Hippo in Fourth-century north Africa. The central tenets of the discipline take seriously the reality of sin in the world (and thus the imperfectability of human creation), the moral freedom of people to both believe and to act, and the ethically binding principle of the New Testament "Royal Law" (cf. Matt. 22:35–40, Mark 12:28–34 and Luke 10:25–28). Niebuhr's classic explication remain his 1939 Gifford Lectures, published dually as *The Nature and Destiny of Man, Vol 1: Human Nature: A Christian Interpretation* and *Vol 2: Human Destiny: A Christian Interpretation* (New York: Charles Scribner's Sons, 1964). For a contemporary explication of the broader principles of Christian Realism, see Eric Patterson, "Eight Principles for Christian Realism," PROVIDENCE online, 23 Sept 2020, at Eight Principles for Christian Realism—Providence.

2 This is a phrase which the U.S. Army Chaplain Corps formerly used to elucidate its mission to advise commands on the moral and ethical demands of the profession of arms. More recently, the branch more banally terms this as "moral advisement." See FM 16–1, *Religious Support* (Washington, DC: HQDA, 21 JAN 2019): 1–3.

3 James Dubik has rightly called for American strategic military leaders to be more attuned to the language, thought processes, and advisement mechanisms of the civilian political class which governs the nation's use of force. See his *Just War Reconsidered: Strategy, Ethics, and Theory* (Lexington, KY: University Press of Kentucky Press, 2016), 137–172.

4 I am indebted to the late theologian Ronald Thiemann for providing me this construct. See my Unpublished Ph.D. Dissertation, *Marginality as Power: The Ecclesiology of Dietrich Bonhoeffer as a Construct for Public Theology Through the United States Army Chaplain Corps*, Lampeter, Wales; University of Wales Trinity Saint David (2015), 191.

Chapter 1

1 Office of the Director of National Intelligence, *Annual Threat Assessment of the U.S. Intelligence Community* (Washington, DC: ODNI, 5 February 2024), available online at ATA-2024-Unclassified-Report.pdf.

2 Jane Harman, Eric Eidelman, et al., *Report of the Commission on the National Defense Strategy* (Washington, DC: The Rand Organization, 29 July 2024), 5, available online at Commission on the National Defense Strategy | RAND.

3 Scholars of war differentiate between both its nature (that which is unchanging over time and is true of war generally in varying contexts and circumstances) and its character (that which changes over time and is attenuated by advances in technology, weaponry, tactics, causal factors of conflicts, etc.). All-domain Operations is the official joint operational doctrine of the United States Department of Defense; see its JP 3–0, *Joint Campaigns and Operations* (Washington, DC: The Joint Staff, 18 June 2022). Doctrinally and conceptually, the U.S. Army now contends that we continually exist in a state of geopolitical competition just below conflict; see its ADP 3–0, *Operations* (Washington, DC: HQ, Department of the Army, 31 July 2019). As an ethicist, I note now that as the Army sees competition as so prevalent—even after war—that it mentions only twice in this keystone doctrinal manual a return to a "lasting, stable peace," though it fails to define or demarcate that concept for the force.

4 This noted, as a Christian Realist, I am placing myself squarely within the vein of those who believe that no state is sacrosanct, and in a fallen world, cannot be imbued with anything beyond penultimate, immanent power under subscribed limits. For a fine analysis of and distinction with the various expressions of Christian Nationalism, see Eric Patterson, "Christian Realism, Christian Nationalism(s), and Religious Freedom," PROVIDENCE online, 12 Dec 2024, at Christian Realism, Nationalism(s), and Religious Freedom—Providence.

5 Saint Augustine, *City of God*, ed. Etienne Gibson and trans. Gerald G. Walsh, et. al. (New York: Image Books, 1958); 456. For a classic understanding of the restoration of peace as the teleological *raison d'etre* of war and harmonization of society, see George Weigel, *Tranquillitas Ordinis: The Present and Future Promise of American Catholic Thought on War and Peace* (New York: Oxford University Press, 1987).

6 Organizational theorists describe a "wicked problem" as one with multi-causal factors and solution sets, which in their solving, then beget other, unforeseen problem. The origin of this synonymous term is from Horst W.J. Rittel and Melvin M. Weber, "Planning Problems Are Wicked Problem," in *Developments in Design Methodology*, ed. Nigel Cross (Chichester, NY: John Wiley & Sons, 1984), 135–144.

7 Military strategists and planners frame war at the tactical (local), operational (regional and theater) and strategic (nation-state, global, and even extra-terrestrial) levels.

8 To be fair, however, my early attempts at healing from 2011–2013 were fraught with the same challenges of many veterans, including being over-medicated, misdiagnosed and unheard by a phalanx of clinical providers. However, since then, the systemic growth in knowledge of the military clinical and therapeutic professions in treating both PTSD and TBI has been immense, as evidenced by the world-leading research and treatment at the National Intrepid Center of Excellence, both at Walter Reed National Military Medical Center in Bethesda, MD and Brooke Army Medical Center in San Antonio, TX.

9 Larry Kent Graham, *Moral Injury: Restoring Wounded Souls* (Nashville: Abingdon Press, 2017), 77.

10 This will follow in the next chapter when I discuss the concept of ontology, or being, for the warrior.

11 Simon Edwards, *Soldier of Hope: Lessons from the International Community in Recovery and Growth from Battlefield Trauma and Mental Health* (London: The Winston Churchill Memorial Trust, 2016), 27.

12 Ethicists generally break the discipline down into metaphysical, normative, and applied ethics, the latter corelating moral norms with ethical behaviors and actions. In the military, warriors tend to instinctively gravitate towards this latter concept, placing a premium on discovering right behavior or action in morally ambiguous and ethically complex dilemmas, yet often without first examining their own or the organization's paradigmatic values, principles, and beliefs.

13 For a searing, poignant account of the enduring moral cost of such sacrificial service in war, I am drawn to that of my late colleague in the Army chaplaincy, CH (COL) Herm Keizer, who was instrumental in the founding of the Soul Repair Center at Brite Divinity School in Fort Worth, TX. Herm's story is lovingly captured by Rita Nakashima Brock and Gabriella Lettini in *Soul Repair: Recovering from Moral Injury After War* (Boston: Beacon Press, 2012), 22–28, 55–57, and 77–81.

14 Jonathan Shay, *Achilles in Vietnam: Combat Trauma and the Undoing of Character* (New York: Scribner, 1994) and *Odysseus in America: Combat Trauma and the Trials of Homecoming* (New York: Scribner, 2002).

15 While in no way endorsing self-harm, I note that my students have particularly resonated with Sophocles's character of Aias. In that play, Aias (often wrongly transliterated in English as Ajax) undergoes a tortuous moral self-assessment after combat and decides to commit suicide over his perceived failure to uphold his (and his family's) honor and so to dishonor his country. See Sophocles, *Oedipus the King and Other Tragedies: Oedipus the King, Aias, Philoctetes, Oedipus at Colonus* (Oxford: Oxford University Press, 2015): 77–138.

16 Jonathan Shay, "Moral Injury," in *Psychoanalytic Psychology* 31/2 (2014): 182–191. Theologian Joseph McDonald has rightly termed Shay's as "The Betrayal Model," one of the two dominant definitions in the scholarly and practical literature around moral injury. See his "What is Moral Injury?," in *Moral Injury A Guidebook for Understanding and Engagement*, ed. Brad E. Kelle (Lantham, MD: Lexington Books, 2020), 10–11.

17 For the clinical criteria and definition of PTSD, see American Psychiatric Association, "Definition of Posttraumatic Stress Disorder," in *Diagnostic and Statistical Manual of Mental Disorders* (DSM-5), 1st. ed. (Washington, DC: American Psychiatric Publishing, 2013), 265; 271–280.

18 Shay (1994), 1–22.

19 Ibid., 23–38.

20 Shay (1994), 5–6.

21 Ed Tick, *War and the Soul: Healing Our Nation's Veterans from Posttraumatic Stress Disorder* (Wheaton, IL: Quest Publishing, 2005), 104.

22 Larry Dewey, *War and Redemption: Treatment and Recovery in Combat-related Posttraumatic Stress Disorder* (Burlington, VT: Ashgate Publishing Co., 2004), 9–17, 73–96, 201–228.

23 Cf. endnote no. 19. However, the VOA has expanded the fundraising appeal towards moral injury with a recent series of repeating, full-page, color advertisements in major American newspapers such as in *The Wall Street Journal*, Thursday, 8 September 2022, pg. A6B. Without mentioning others, I can say that both I and several fellow professionals in the field of moral injury are deeply concerned about this development, as it raises the question of whose interests are being pursued through such a campaign.

24 Cf. Shay, endnote no. 20. However, within the ethics community of the profession of arms, none has more repeatedly sounded a note of concern about the *effect* on the profession by such a diminished capacity for moral reflectivity in its practitioners than has Don Snider. In his estimation, there is no greater danger to the profession (and by derivation to the American Republic) than for its professionals to become morally and ethically unreflective and yet to still wield the immense power which the nation has entrusted to them. See his Don M. Snider, "The U.S. Army as Profession," in *The Future of the Army Profession*, 2nd ed., ed. Lloyd J. Matthews (New York: McGraw-Hill, 2005), 1–17 and more recently, Don M. Snider, "Will Army 2025 be a Military Profession?" in *Parameters* 45/4 (2015): 39–51, DOI:10.55540/ 0031–1723.2985.

25 McDonald (2020; 8–10, further terms this "The Perpetration Model." However, his coinage of this tittle is based off an earlier version of the Litz definition from 2009, and I argue that the definition cited here from 2016 is the more consistent one that has settled into the scholarly and practical discourse on moral injury, hence I would term this "The Transgression Model."

26 Shira Maguen and Brett Litz, "Moral Injury in the Context of War," U.S. Department of Veterans Affairs National Center for PTSD, online at http://www.ptsd.va.gov/professional/co-occurring/moral_injury_at_war.asp.

27 Timothy Mallard. "Twin Children of the Great War: Assessing the Effects of Moral and Spiritual Injury Today," in *A Persistent Fire: The Strategic Ethical Impact of World War I on the Global Profession of Arms*, eds. Timothy S. Mallard and Nathan H. White (Washington, DC: National Defense University Press, 2020), 273–295.

28 Graham (2017), 13, delineates between "agential moral injury" (that which one does to another) and "receptive moral injury" (that which one has done to one by another). Graham, however, is a pastoral theologian and is principally writing to clergy, counsellors, and chaplains working in the field of pastoral counselling, and

not as an ethicist. Thus, his utilization of these two discrete concepts—laudable in their attempt to capture the criticality of moral agency—is not generally known outside his field and would not find currency within normative ethics. For the latter, including important derivative discussions of moral disposition, capacity, judgment, psycho-cognitive development in persons, and the impact of social theory and cultural values, see Thomas W. Ogletree, "Agents and Moral Formation," in *The Blackwell Companion to Religious Ethics*, ed. William Schweiker (Oxford: Blackwell Publishing, 2005), 36–44.

29 On the healthy functioning of social institutions, including confessional religious belief systems, see James H. Burtness, *Consequences: Morality, Ethics and the Future* (Minneapolis: Augsburg Fortress Press, 1999), 27, and Tom Beauchamp, *Philosophical Ethics: An Introduction to Moral Philosophy* (New York: McGraw-Hill Publishers, 1982), 21.

30 In Augustine's taxonomy, *agere sequitur esse* ("doing follows being"). To be sure, in our often spiritually apathetic and indifferent contemporary culture it has almost become *de rigueur* to propose that moral leadership in a democratic polity can be (and for some proponents must be) divorced from any religious or spiritual moorings, but that remains a tendentious and illogical point. In essence, we must divorce from our analysis of moral injury as a phenomenon any type of political ideology or philosophy which seeks to incorporate a public policy agenda that may cloud how we respond to and treat any injury to the warrior arising from combat (for example, the contemporary attempts in America by both secularists or atheists to limit the First Amendment right of the free exercise of religious belief). Said differently, the late Fr. Richard John Neuhaus was decidedly correct in asserting that either religion must have a place in the public square, or the democratic project is in peril. See his Richard J. Neuhaus, *The Naked Public Square: Religion and Democracy in America* (Grand Rapids: Eerdmans, 1988). Another compelling voice on this point was from the dissident Alexander Solzhenitsyn, who warned of the social dissolution occurring in modernity from our impoverished collective soul. See his commencement address to Harvard University, "The Exhausted West," in *Harvard Magazine* 80/6 (July–August 1978).

31 A point within military leader development repeatedly emphasized by former Commandant of the U.S. Marine Corps, Gen. Charles C. Krulak, Jr. See his "Plenary Remarks on Integrity and Leadership," at the JSCOPE Conference, Washington, DC (27 Jan 2000).

32 Definition, The International Centre for Moral Injury, online at What is Moral Injury?—Durham University.

33 Mallard (2020); 282.

34 For instance and towards clarity, see the proposal to codify moral injury as a disorder in Tyler J. VanderWeele, Wortham J. S., Carey L. B., Case, B. W., Cowden, R. G., Duffee C, Jackson-Meyer ,K., Lu, F., Mattson, S. A., Padgett, R. N., Peteet J. R., Rutledge, J., Symons, X., and Koenig, H. G. (2025) "Moral trauma, moral distress,

moral injury, and moral injury disorder: definitions and assessments." *Front. Psychol.* 16:1422441. DOI: online at https://10.3389/fpsyg.2025.1422441.

35 In conversation with clinical professionals on this point, many have here raised two principal objections (e.g., that to precisely prescribe what moral injury is will either): 1) lead to a categorization of diagnostic criteria in reference texts and/or clinical curricula, or 2) lead to a subsequent effect of establishing and concretizing a trend of diagnostic praxis by medical or clinical experts and practitioners. For some, the first possibility might negate the current focus in moral injury studies on the primacy of the individual while the second possibility might lead to an unhealthful application of monetary benefits to a malady which, with care and patience, can be rectified. Both points have some legitimacy, but they only support my larger contention that the debate about moral injury needs to be brought more fully into the professional discourse outside the clinical professions, to now include theological ethicists, moral philosophers, chaplains, and clergy, and as I am referencing here, military professionals.

36 There are, however, non-Western voices who are advancing a call to freshly apply moral injury in the communal context, particularly relative to the shared pain, memories, narratives and art, and evocations of hope in marginalized people groups. See Assala Khettache, "The Weaponization of Collective Moral Injuries in Africa," the 2024 Robbins Lecture, the International Centre for Moral Injury, Durham, UK. Note that her work particularly critiques the rise and exploitation of such narratives by the Putin regime through the paramilitary, Wagner Group. Regarding this group and its tactics, see John Lechner, *Death is Our Business: Russian Mercenaries and the New Era of Private Warfare* (New York: Bloomsbury Publishing, 2025).

37 For example, as with President Truman's senior political, scientific, and military advisors and their internal policy debate about the moral legitimacy, military efficacy, and strategic advisability to drop both United States' atomic bombs on Hiroshima and Nagasaki, Japan on 6 and 9 August 1945, respectively. See the trove of declassified, publicly available memoranda, notes, letters, and statements behind this process from the Harry S. Truman Presidential Library, online at The Decision to Drop the Atomic Bomb | Harry S. Truman. For a recent ethical analysis of this fateful decision relative only to the employment of the first weapon, see Marc LiVecche, "Military Necessity as Imperative: Just War and Hiroshima," in *Military Necessity and Just War Statecraft: The Principle of National Security Stewardship*, eds. Eric Patterson and Marc LiVecche (London: Routledge, 2023).

38 RADM Joyce Johnson, D.O., "Moral Injury," in *Military Officer* (July 2017), 48.

39 Sacks, following George Bernard Shaw, was militating against an ethic in which anyone fully places the moral risk of a decision onto another without assuming any responsibility themselves, and concomitantly thus increases collective risk taking. See his *Morality: Restoring the Common Good in Trying Times* (New York: Basic Books, 2020), 92–94.

40 A consistent stream of scholarship supporting the integration of spirituality into the clinical treatment of moral injury has arisen in Australia and its military forces,

particularly its chaplaincies. Though I disagree with their suggestion that moral injury should be codified in the next edition of the Diagnostic and Statistical Manual for Clinical Disorders, I find much to admire in a recent paper by Mark Layson and Lindsay Carey, "Moral Injury Narratives and the Role of Chaplains in the Australian Context: A Bio-Psycho-Social-Spiritual Approach to Prevention and Treatment," Paper Presentation at the International Centre for Moral Injury Annual Conference, Durham, UK, 22–24 April 2024.

41 For all the above suggestions, see ethicist Duncan MacIntosh, "Posttraumatic Stress Disorder Weaponized: A Theory of Moral Injury?" in Justin T. McDaniel (ed.), *Preventing and Treating the Invisible Wounds of War: Combat Trauma, Moral Injury, and Psychological Health* (Oxford: Oxford University Press,), 175–206.

42 Khettache (2024).

43 Cf. endnote no. 1.

44 A point of clarification is in order here. Values, principles, and beliefs are not synonymous as discrete terms. However, taken as a whole, they can capture the inner ethical basis of either an individual or group that form the core of a moral foundation. For instance, one will often hear in colloquial discourse, particularly in the profession of arms, about following one's "moral compass," usually without any further delineation as to what constitutes the components of such an instrument in the metaphor (e.g. what makes up either the arms, the face, or especially magnetic north). Thus, throughout this book, these terms are used in the aggregate to refer to the notion that either a person or a group can and should have a well-defined and decided upon moral foundation comprising these elements, particularly as this is crucial to correlating the same with duty in war. For a helpful exploration of how these relate to both consequentialism and non-consequentialism as well as discerning action in applied ethics, see Philip Petit, "Consequentialism," and Michael Smith, "Realism," both in *A Companion to Ethics*, Peter Singer (ed.) (Oxford: Blackwell Publishing, 1993), 231–240 and 399–410 respectively.

45 Mallard (2020).

46 Many of the thoughts for this chapter arise from a co-presentation of the author with Dr. Brian Powers to St. Chad's College and Durham University on Remembrance Day 2024, entitled "Moral Injury in Recent and Future Conflicts." Powers rightly notes that, for one suffering moral injury, one directs the first two of these emotions inwardly towards the self while directing the latter two outwardly towards others.

47 In comparison and particularly in the wake of the physical, emotional, mental, familial and social corrosion occasioned by COVID-19, suicide as a cause of death in the United States nationally reached its highest level in 2023 since the beginning of World War II. See Julie Wernau, "U.S. Suicides Reached a Record High Last Year," in *The Wall Street Journal*, 29 November 2023. However, and comparatively against the U.S. populace in 2021 (also measuring the first full year of data after COVID-19), while the age-and-sex adjusted rate of completed suicide for the United States

increased by 4.5% that year, that same rate for post-uniformed Veterans increased by 11.6% that year. See U.S. Department of Veterans Affairs, *2023 National Veteran Suicide Prevention Annual Report* (Washington, DC: Office of Mental Health and Suicide Prevention, 1 November 2023).

48 MacIntosh (2023), 176.

49 John Mark Mattox, "The Moral Foundations of Army Officership," in *the Future of the Army Profession*, 2nd ed., ed. Lloyd J. Matthews (New York: McGraw-Hill Publishing, 2005), 387–408.

50 Shay (1994); 33–34, further states that this phenomenon in individual warriors leads to a subsequent corrosion of social trust amongst the body politic. Again Sacks (2020); 94, concurs, and believes that this reinforces the collective move of "we" to "I" that dominates the western *zeitgeist.* Socially, Sacks argues that for western cultures to return to health, this process must be reversed.

51 Notwithstanding the senseless criminal deaths of the prisoners therein, for a rending account of moral injury—and I would contend deep spiritual injury—in the life of one American veteran of that prison, SGT Joshua Casteel, see Jennifer Percy, "The Priest of Abu Ghraib," in *The Smithsonian* 49/9 (January-February 2019): 44–55. Regarding the broader professional effect of moral corrosion due to war in the American leadership of the profession of arms, see Tom Vanden Brook, "Senior Military Officials Sanctioned for More Than 500 Cases of Serious Misconduct," in *USA Today* Online (24 October 2017), at https://www.usatoday.com/story/news/politics/2017/10/24/generals-sex-misconduct-pentagon-army-sanctions-hagel-gillibrand/794770001/.

52 Ibid Vanden Brook but see also Charles D. Allen and William G. Braun, "Trust: Implications for the Army Profession," in *Military Review* (September-October 2013); 73–85. Here, I intentionally do not mention the catastrophic effect on the moral *ethos* of the United States Navy from the so-called "Fat Leonard" Scandal, not because I wish to ignore it but because the scandal is still being played out in both military and civilian courts, even after over two decades of investigation and prosecution. For a summary of this scandal even touching on its moral injury to the Navy and that service's organizational deficiencies, see Grant Ryan and Brant Hipple, "Fat Leonard Still Weighs on WestPac Logistics," in *Proceedings* 150/11/1,461, U.S. Naval Institute (November 2024), online at Fat Leonard Still Weighs on WestPac Logistics | Proceedings—November 2024 Vol. 150/11/1,461.

53 Roméo Dallaire, *Shake Hands with the Devil: the Failure of Humanity in Rwanda* (London: Arrow Books, 2004).

54 Eric James Szandzik, "President Clinton's Nonintervention in the Rwanda Genocide: An Analysis of U.S. Presidential Foreign Policy Decisions," in *World Affairs* 185/1 (2022); 176–206, online at https://doi.org/10.1177/00438200211064941.

55 Ibid, 191. Note Szandzik's summary judgment that President Clinton's nonintervention decision in Rwanda cannot be dismissed due to pending geopolitical

commitments in Bosnia, as he writes: "...Clinton's nonintervention in Rwanda... reflected an unwillingness to manage multiple foreign policy challenges at the expense of his domestic priorities."

56 The Responsibility to Protect was initially codified in a document by the same name from the Canadian-led International Commission on Intervention and State Sovereignty (ICISS) in 2001, largely catalysed by BG Dallaire's experience. However, the doctrine has now been organizationally codified in the United Nations and given transnational geopolitical status as a viable military response option. See the United Nations page online at About the Responsibility to Protect | United Nations. The problem of employing R2P (at least at the UN level) is that the Security Council requires unanimity in its vote to authorize the option, a necessary precursor to deploying and employing any military force to prevent genocide. Thus, the same lack of political authorities which constrained BG Dallaire's force in Rwanda in 1994 largely remain an unresolved problem today.

57 U.S. Army Peacekeeping and Stability Operations Institute, *Mass Atrocity Prevention and Response Options: A Policy Planning Handbook* (Carlisle, PA: PKSOI, 2012), online at MAPRO_handbook_final.pdf.

58 I have no analysis to prove this, but I believe that my late friend Sen. Max Cleland catalysed this turn in American political life when he was appointed by President Jimmy Carter as the Administrator of Veterans Affairs in 1977. Max, a triple amputee and recipient of the Silver Star for combat valor in Vietnam, was a visible example to all Americans at the presidential cabinet level of the cost of that war, and I think that in his public leadership he socialized the nation's acceptance of his fellow veterans. Later a U.S. Senator from the state of Georgia, Max personally and consistently encouraged me to pursue healing from the internal wounds of war, which he always contended were far more difficult to overcome than even the life-altering physical injuries he sustained. See his *Strong at the Broken Places* (Waco, TX: Word Books, 1980). On this journey towards personal healing, I must also thank my good friend Dave Roever, who like Max was badly wounded in Vietnam and, also like him, who consistently and lovingly prompted me to seek a full healing in God, both body and soul.

59 Leonard Wong and Steven J. Gerras. *Veteran Disability Compensation and the Army Profession: Good Intentions Gone Awry* (Carlisle, PA: U.S. Army War College Press, 29 Jan 2021), online at Veteran Disability Compensation and the Army Profession: Good Intentions Gone Awry.

Chapter 2

1 Nigel Biggar, "What Should Christian Ethics Learn from World War I?", in *A Persistent Fire: The Strategic Ethical Impact of World War I on the Global Profession of Arms*, eds. Timothy S. Mallard and Nathan H. White (Washington, DC: National Defense University Press, 2020), 1–20. Note particularly here Biggar's assertion—made to a conference composed of both academic ethicists and military professionals—that it

is indeed both possible and right for the Christian concept of self-giving love to walk the battlefield.

2 These instruments of national power, the so-called 'hard power' rubric colloquially known by its acronym of DIME-FIL, contrast with Joseph Nye's concept of a nation's 'soft power.' Nye notes that this power "...can rest on such resources as the attraction of one's ideas or on the ability to set the political agenda in a way that shapes the preferences others express" and that this exercise of influence "tends to be associated with intangible power resources such as culture, ideology, and institutions." However, the totality of a nation's power is not in either hard or soft power but in its aggregation of both in pursuit of balanced national security ends, ways, and means. See Nye's original concept in his *Understanding International Conflicts: An Introduction to Theory and History* (New York: Longman, 2003); 60. More recently and in assessment of the Trump Administration's reversion solely to 'hard power,' see Nye, "Is This the End of Soft Power?" *Financial Times* (8–9 March 2025); FT Weekend 1–2.

3 Thomas Farr, "Theology and International Religious Liberty," Plenary Remarks to the Christianity and National Security Conference 2017, Washington, DC, online at Thomas Farr Christianity & National Security 2017: Theology & International Religious Liberty - Providence. Some may contest Farr's assessment based on the passage of the International Religious Freedom Act of 1998, which established an Ambassador-at-Large for International Religious Freedom at the Department of States, founded the U.S. Commission on International Religious Freedom (USCIRF), and mandated an annual report from USCIRF to the Congress and President on the statute's subject, an assessment which famously and annually lists "Countries of Particular Concern" on this value. However, in Farr's estimate, both the ambassadorial position (and supporting staff) and the report have failed to centrally integrate religious freedom as an enduring *policy* priority across presidential administrations as a core United States national value. For a review of USCIRF's work and its current report on international religious freedom, see their 2024 Annual Report online at Annual Reports | USCIRF.

4 Marshall spoke in the gender conventions of his time, but his observations hold whether considering either male or female warriors; indeed, the soul knows no gender. Moreover, the timelessness of his words ring especially true in reminding us that the question of technology and humanity in war is neither new nor novel, which Marshall certainly saw firsthand as a major in the American Expeditionary Force in World War I. Finally, while this same quotation is often cited in Marshall's later acceptance speech for the Nobel Peace Prize in 1953, its genesis is here. See George C. Marshall, *The Papers of George Catlett Marshall,* eds. Larry I. Bland, Sharon Ritenour Stevens, and Clarence E. Wunderlin, Jr. (Lexington, VA.: The George C. Marshall Foundation, 1981–). Electronic version based on *The Papers of George Catlett Marshall,* vol. 2, *"We Cannot Delay," July 1, 1939-December 6, 1941* (Baltimore and London: The Johns Hopkins University Press, 1986), 534–538.

5 Most recently, the U.S. military services have produced separate efforts towards linking spirituality and readiness. The U.S. Army published official doctrine which only

added (after initial fielding to the force) a section on "Spiritual Readiness" as one of five readiness domains, thus the doctrine functionally sees spirituality only as a utilitarian good facilitating combat readiness. See FM 7–22, C1, *Holistic Health and* Fitness (Washington, DC: HQ Department of the Army, 8 October 2020). For the U.S. Navy and in like philosophical framework as the Army, it has fielded its *Warrior Toughness Readiness Guide*, which incorporates an undefined rubric of "Mind, Body, and Soul" and which defines 'Spiritual Toughness' as "…a product of reflection, awareness, and commitment to something greater than one's self propelling them to prepare and execute with conviction." This document is part of a larger suite of training materials published as part of the *Forged by the Sea Culture of Readiness Program 2.0* (Washington, DC: U.S. Navy Culture and Force Resilience Office, March 2024). For earlier joint force efforts towards this goal, see Patrick J. Sweeney, Jeffrey E. Rhodes, and Bruce Boling, "Spiritual Fitness: A Key Component of Total Force Fitness," in *Joint Forces Quarterly* 66/3rd Quarter (2012); 35–41 and Patrick J. Sweeney and Louis W. Fry, "Character Development Through Spiritual Leadership," in *Consulting Psychology Journal: Practice and Research* 64/2 (2012): 89–107.

6 Nathan Wheeler, "For a Holy Priesthood: A Petrine Model for Evangelical Cultural Engagement," in *Journal of the Evangelical Theological Society* 59/3 (September 2016): 523–539. Wheeler convincingly argues that by such a sacrificial ethic the church takes on the responsibility to become the vessel of "redemptive responsibility for the godliness of the world." However, even more important is the Christological model for Christians to engage in this self-giving ethic, which Dietrich Bonhoeffer expressed in his later concept of "Jesus, the man for others" (*Jesus, die Mensch für die anderen*) in *Letters and Papers from Prison, DBWE,* Vol. 8, ed. John W. de Gruchy and trans. Isabel Best, Lisa E. Dahill, Reinhard Krauss, and Nancy Lukens (Minneapolis: Fortress Press, 2009), 501.

7 See again Shay (2003), Tick (2005), and Dewey (2004), especially. A type of social nihilism, as I term it, is more indicative of both moral but especially spiritual injury in the post-modern ethos of the Millennial Generation and GenZ. For how this reality pervades American Millennial warriors (who ironically also often exhibit an intense interest in spirituality), see Stephen Mansfield, *The Faith of the American Soldier* (New York: Tarcher Press, 2005); 36–39. For a fine theological exploration of the moral risk to the warrior for reflective capacity, see Marc LiVecche, "The Fifth Image: Seeing the Enemy With Just War Eyes," in *PROVIDENCE* 1/4 (Summer 2016): 50–56.

8 Elliot Ackerman, "The Danger Posed by Today's Angry Vets," in *The Wall Street Journal*, 10 January 2025, online at The Danger Posed by Today's Angry Vets - WSJ.

9 My thought has been particularly shaped by the work of post-World War II European intellectuals, who in helping their societies recover from that cataclysm, faced the daunting prospect of both engendering renewed faith in effecting comprehensive healing in those they served. Two of the finest exemplars in this process were the German Pastor Helmut Thielicke and the Swiss Psychiatrist Paul Tournier. For the former, see his *How to Believe Again* (Minneapolis: Fortress Press, 1972) and for the

latter see his *The Whole Person in a Broken World*, transl. John and Helen Doberstein (New York: Harper & Row, 1964) amongst their many compelling works.

10 Martin Thornton, *English Spirituality: An Outline of Ascetical Theology According to the English Pastoral Tradition* (Cambridge, MA: Cowley Publications, 1986); 35. For a recent Biblical exposition of Trinitarian Christian ontology, including a healthy dualism between present and future, see Graham Tomlin, *The Prodigal Spirit: The Trinity, the Church and the Future of the World* (London: Alpha International, 2011); 44–45.

11 Harold G. Koenig, Tyler J. VanderWeele, and John R. Peteet, "Understanding the Religion-Physical Health Relationship," in *Handbook of Religion and Health*, 3rd Ed. (Oxford: Oxford University Press, 2024); 611–626. This latest edition posits the criticality of how religion and spirituality—whether from a monotheistic, Eastern, or even secular model—becomes a predictor of increased individual physical health, resilience, and longevity, as well as social cohesion and communal strength.

12 Lindsay Carey, et. al., "Moral Injury, Spiritual Care and the Role of Chaplains: An Exploratory Scoping Review of Literature and Resources," in *Journal of Religion and Health* 55/14 (August 2016); 1218–1245. Berg's original 1992 internet-based definition is unavailable, but he replicates it in a later article entitled "The Use of the Computer as a Tool for Assessment and Research in Pastoral Care," in *Journal of Healthcare Chaplaincy* 6/1 (1994); 11–25, DOI online at https://doi.org/10.1300/J080v06n01_03.

13 Though Carey cites him, the full reference for him is ,J. E. Fuson, "A Pastoral Counselling Model for Leading Post-Combat Christian Soldiers Experiencing Spiritual Injury to Spiritual Health Through Examining the Biblical Concepts of Evil, Pain, Abandonment, and Forgiveness." Biola University (2013) ProQuest Dissertation and Theses, 1303015706; vi.

14 Several years ago, I provided an initial definition of spiritual injury, that it is (to wit): "...the intra- and inter-personal damage to souls brought on by significant trauma, including the rupture to foundational religious values, beliefs and attitudes, the inability to healthfully participate in an immanent human faith community, and the temporary or permanent loss of a transcendent relationship to God (manifested particularly in questions about forgiveness, doubt, truth, meaning, and hope)." However, and through the patient critique of many scholars, practitioners, and students, I came to see that this definition: 1) while having a secondary subject lacked a primary subject (as per my observations around the present definitions of moral injury); 2) attempted to be too descriptive and without demonstrating cause and effect, and; 3) was simply too verbose to be routinely internalized and understood. See Mallard (2020); 275.

15 Brian Powers, "Christian Theology and Moral Injury," in *Moral Injury: A Guidebook for Understanding and Engagement*, ed. Brad Kelle (London: Roman & Littlefield, 2020), 191. For a fuller treatment of Powers's exploration of the fullness of Augustinian theology to moral injury, particularly in war, see his *Full Darkness:*

Original Sin, Moral Injury, and Wartime Violence (Grand Rapids, MI: William. B. Eerdmans, 2019).

16 Mallard (2020), 294.

17 For a compelling fictional account of how, for a warrior, both moral and spiritual injury become lived realities after combat, see William Brodrick, *The Discourtesy of Death* (New York: The Overlook Press, 2013). In this story, Michael (a former British Lieutenant in Northern Ireland in the Troubles) contrasts with his brother Nigel, an Anglican Priest, who had once delivered a decisive sermon on duty in war to Michael's regiment. The voice Michael hears at the point of action reflects his foundational faith and moral conflict, and mirrors that heard by the Prophet Elijah in the cave while fleeing King Ahab (1 Kings 19:9–15).

18 Note the wisdom of Dietrich Bonhoeffer, when at even a young age, he opined, "What one understands about person and community simultaneously makes a decisive statement about the concept of God. The concepts of person, community, and God are inseparably and essentially interrelated." See Dietrich Bonhoeffer, *Sanctorum Communio: A Theological Study of the Sociology of the Church*, ed. by Clifford Green and trans.by Reinhard Krauss and Nancy Lukens (Minneapolis: Fortress Press, 1998), 33–34.

19 Here, I am following the pioneering work of Dr. Murray Bowen and his concept of the family as a system which works around eight inter-connected concepts (triangles; differentiation of self; nuclear family emotional process; family projection process; multigenerational transmission process; emotional cutoff; sibling position, and; societal emotional process). This concept continues to shape marriage and family therapy today, and its work remains shaped by The Bowen Center for the Study of the Family, which notes: "Families so profoundly affect their members' thoughts, feelings, and actions that it often seems as if people are living under the same "emotional skin." People solicit each other's attention, approval, and support, and they react to each other's needs, expectations, and upsets. This connectedness and reactivity make the functioning of family members interdependent. A change in one person's functioning is predictably followed by reciprocal changes in the functioning of others. Families differ somewhat in their degree of interdependence, but it is always present to some degree." See that center's website at Introduction to the Eight Concepts—The Bowen Center for the Study of the Family.

20 Ernest Hemingway, "Soldier's Home," in *The Complete Short Stories of Ernest Hemingway: The Finca Gigía Edition* (New York: Charles Scribner's Sons,1987) 111–116.

21 As a rule from my military pastoral experience, for complete reintegration to occur in healthy family systems, I worked from a 1 to 3 model, meaning that if a deployment were a total separation of 12 months, it will generally take a total of 36 months for healthy rebalancing to occur. Mind, this can be often attenuated by a number of complicating factors, such as: extensive pre-combat separations for pre-deployment

unit training which lengthen total separation; rapid post-combat military requirements for a warrior's posting to a new duty station; the warrior's possible experience of lingering physical and mental woundedness from war; marital discord; and new and pressing requirements of others within the family system or even extended family (for example, adolescent teens in emotional crisis or aging, perhaps ill, parents or grandparents needing family support).

22 Mallard (2020), 285.

23 Tick (2005), 104.

24 Mallard (2020: 286–287. See also the evocative (but truncated) suggestion of ecclesial communities to embody this in Brett T. Litz, Leslie Lebowitz, Matt J. Gray, and William P. Nash in *Adaptive Disclosure A New Treatment for Military Trauma, Loss, and Moral Injury* (New York: The Guilford Press, 2016), 126.

25 Koenig, et. al. (2024), 626.

26 Martin Marty, *Politics, Religion, and the Common Good* (San Francisco: Jossey-Bass, 2000); 50–51.

Chapter 3

1 Cf. endnote no. 7.

2 Many of the thoughts for this chapter arise from a co-presentation of the author with Dr. Brian Powers to St. Chad's College and Durham University on Remembrance Day 2024, entitled "Moral Injury in Recent and Future Conflicts."

3 Walter Russel Mead, "Trump Faces a Different World in Term Two," *The Wall Street* Journal (11 NOV 2024), online at Trump Faces a Different World in Term Two - WSJ. Also, note John Nagl and George Topic, "On (Protracted) War: The Challenge of Sustained Large-Scale Combat Operations," *Modern War Institute at West Point* (9 OCT 2024), online at On (Protracted) War: The Challenge of Sustained Large-Scale Combat Operations—Modern War Institute.

4 Arthur F. Lykke, Jr., "Defining Military Strategy," in *Military Review* (January–February 1997): 183–186. Note, however, that Lykke explicitly does not correlate this model to a nation defining grand strategy; that is a separate process altogether.

5 As quoted by Craig Whitlock in his brilliant book *The Afghanistan Papers: A Secret History of the War* (New York: Simon & Schuster, 2022); 105. Note that Whitlock bases his work principally on a review of the quarterly and annual reporting work of the congressionally mandated Office of the Special Inspector General for Afghanistan Reconstruction (SIGAR), which reports to the Inspectors General of the United States Department of Defense, Department of State, and the U.S. Agency for International Development. The SIGAR mission will conclude in 2025, but its work can be viewed online at SIGAR—Home.

6 Todd Greentree, "What Went Wrong in Afghanistan?" in *Parameters* 51/4 (Winter 2021–2022): 7–21 and Whitlock (2021), 103–114.

7 Jamie Shea, "NATO Withdraws from Afghanistan: Short-term and Long-term Consequences for the Western Alliance" (#Critical Thinking, Friends of Europe, September 3, 2021).

8 BBC News, "Bagram: Last U.S. and NATO Forces Leave Key Afghanistan Base," (2 July 2021), online at Bagram: Last US and Nato forces leave key Afghanistan base —BBC News.

9 Ibid Whitlock (2021) and Greentree (2021–2022).

10 Margherita Stancati and Jessica Donati, "Former Afghan Female Troops Live in Fear," in *The Wall Street Journal* (December 29, 2021), A11.

11 Ibid (2005) Mattox.

12 Ibid Allen and Braun (2013). However, this is also the stated value for the U.S. Department of Defense in how American forces are supposed to conduct joint operations with allied and partner nation forces in all-domain operations. See The Chairman of the Joint Chiefs of Staff, *JP 3–0, Joint Operations*, C1 (Washington, DC: U.S. Department of Defense, 22 October 2018), 1–8 and 1–10.

13 H.R. McMaster, "Honor Veterans by Having the Will to Win a War," in *The Wall Street Journal* (10 November 2021), online at Honor Veterans by Having the Will to Win a War—WSJ.

14 Annika Ganzeveld, et. al., "Iran Update" (7 JAN 2025), *The Institute for the Study of War*, online at Iran Update, January 7, 2025 | Institute for the Study of War.

15 See Eliot A. Cohen, "Khomeini Loses Everything," *The Atlantic* (8 DEC 2024), online at Khamenei Loses Everything - The Atlantic and Sune Engel Rasmussen, "Iran Suffers Blow of 'Historic Proportions' with Assad's Fall," *The Wall Street Journal* (10 DEC 2024), online at Iran Suffers Blow of 'Historic Proportions' With Assad's Fall in Syria - WSJ.

16 Angelica Evans, et. al., "Russian Offensive Campaign Assessment (7 JAN 2025), *The Institute for the Study of War*, online at Russian Offensive Campaign Assessment, January 7, 2025 | Institute for the Study of War.

17 Gideon Rose, "Ending War is Hard to Do," in *Foreign Affairs* (21 January 2025), online at Ending War Is Hard to Do: Can Trump Reach Real Settlements in Ukraine and Gaza?

18 Cf. Clausewitz (1973).

19 Tom Galvin, *National Preparedness and Military Readiness: A Primer for Senior Leaders* (Carlisle, PA: The Strategic Studies Institute, 1 Nov 2023), 29–42.

20 HQ, Department of the Army, *ADP 3–0: Operations* (Washington, DC: HQ, Department of the Army, 31 JUL 2019), 1–10.

21 Macubin Owens, "Force Planning: The Crossroads of Strategy and the Political Process," in *Orbis* 59/3 (2015): 411–437.

22 Timothy Mallard, "Strategic Betrayal and the Fall of Afghanistan: Implications for Future War," Paper Presented to the International Network for the Study of War and Religion, the Defence Academy of the United Kingdom, Shrivenham, UK (6 Jul 2022).

23 Omer Bartov, "As a Former IDF Soldier and Historian of Genocide, I Was Deeply Disturbed by my Recent Trip to Israel," *The Guardian* (13 AUG 2024), online at As a former IDF soldier and historian of genocide, I was deeply disturbed by my recent visit to Israel | Israel | The Guardian.

24 Isabel Coles and Ievgeniia Sivorka, "Four Ways Ukraine's Drones Are Changing Warfare," *The Wall Street Journal* (12 OCT 2024), online at Four Ways Ukraine's Drone Innovations Are Changing Warfare—WSJ.

25 Jonathan W. Alexander, "Lethal Autonomous Weapons Systems and the Potential for Moral Injury," Unpublished Ph.D. Dissertation, Salve Regina University ProQuest Dissertations & Theses, 2024. 31636634.

26 Jane Pauley, "Interview with GEN Mark Milley, U.S. Chairman of the Joint Chiefs of Staff," CBS News (10 SEP 2023), online at Watch Sunday Morning: How the U.S. helps pierce the fog of war in Ukraine - Full show on CBS.

27 Heads of State and Government Participating in the Meeting of the North Atlantic Council in Wales, "Wales Summit Declaration," (5 SEP 2014), online at NATO—Official text: Wales Summit Declaration issued by NATO Heads of State and Government (2014), 05–Sep.–2014; Para.14.

28 Gerard Baker, "How American Institutions Went from Trust to Bust," *The Wall Street Journal* (8 SEP 2023). See also the longitudinal decline in American institutions captured in the annual Gallup surveys on the topic at Jeffrey M. Jones, "Confidence in U.S. Institutions Down; Average at New Low," Gallup online, 5 July 2022, at Confidence in U.S. Institutions Down; Average at New Low.

29 Ibid., Gallup (2022), which indicates that though the American military retains a relative positional trust higher than other social institutions (such as the press or the Congress, for example), even the military has been on a gradual but unarguable decline in the public's trust in the past decade.

30 As quoted in Charles D. Allen and William G. Braun, "Trust: Implications for the Army Profession," in *Military Review* (Sep-Oct 2013): 73–85.

31 Carl von Clausewitz, *On War* (Ithaca, NY: Cornell University Press, 1973), 92.

32 Cf. Marc LiVecche, *The Good Kill: Just War and Moral Injury* (Oxford: Oxford University Press, 2021), 148–151. LiVecche specifically argues for the peacetime training and inculcation of virtue in warriors in order to regulate their *in bello* actions and, thus, to blunt their *post bellum* experiences of moral injury. See also Nathan White, "Toward a Resilient Military Ethic," in *A Persistent Fire: The Strategic Ethical Impact of World War I on the Global Profession of Arms*, eds. Timothy S. Mallard and Nathan H. White (Washington, DC: National Defense University Press, 2020), 337–352. White argues that deep resilience in the character of warriors—particularly mentally, emotionally, and spiritually—to the horrors of war is an intentional matter of both personal and organizational training to develop such rigorous inner strength.

Chapter 4

1 For broad reading about the JWT, particularly its history and development leading up to the seven elements listed here, one might begin with Augustine, *City of God*, ed. Etienne Gibson and trans. Gerald G. Walsh, et. al. (New York: Image Books, 1958), 327–328, 446–447, and 452–453; Thomas Aquinas, "Summa Theologiae IIaIIae," in R.W. Dyson, ed., *Aquinas: Political Writings* (Cambridge: University Press, 2002); and Hugo de Grotius, *On the Law of War and Peace* (Whitefish, MT: Kessinger Publishing, 2004), Book III, Chs. 1–22. Regarding the seven major elements presented here, see also Endre Begby, Gregory M. Reichberg, and Henrik Syse, "The Ethics of War, Part II: Contemporary Authors and Issues," in *Philosophy Compass* 7/5 (2012): 328–347, DOI: https://10.1111/j.1747–9991.2011.00476.x.

2 For recent treatments on the growth of the JWT in contemporary war, see James T. Johnson, *Morality and Contemporary Warfare* (New Haven: Yale University Press 2001); Michael Walzer, in both *Arguing About War* (New Haven: Yale University Press, 2005) and *Just and Unjust Wars: A Moral Argument with Historical Illustrations—4th Edition* (New York: Basic Books, 2006); Brian Orend, *The Morality of War* (Peterborough, ONT: Broadview Press, 2006); Martin Cook, "Ethical Issues in War: An Overview," in *The U.S. Army War College Guide to National Security Issues, Vol. II: National Security Policy and Strategy*, ed. J. Boone Bartholomees, 217–227 (Carlisle, PA: Strategic Studies Institute, 2012) and James T. Bretzke, SJ, *Handbook of Roman Catholic Moral Terms* (Washington, DC: Georgetown University Press, 2013).

3 Dubik (2016), 113–136, highlights the capacity of the JWT to be a common framework for both civilian and military leaders to make vital strategic decisions, or what he terms practically "...a performance-oriented, dialogue-execution regime.".

4 LiVecche, *The Good Kill: Just War and Moral Injury*, 176.

5 Victoria J. Barnett, "The Ethics of Care for Civilians, Internally Displaced Persons, and Enemy Prisoners of War," in in *A Persistent Fire: The Strategic Ethical Impact of World War I on the Global Profession of Arms*, eds. Timothy S. Mallard and Nathan H. White (Washington, DC: National Defense University Press, 2020), 159.

6 Office of the High Commissioner for Human Rights, Press Release (7 December 2022), online at UN report details summary executions of civilians by Russian troops in northern Ukraine | OHCHR.

7 Reuters (4 April 2022), online at Russia says footage in Ukraine's Bucha was 'ordered' to blame Russia | Reuters.

8 The International Criminal Court, "Situation in Ukraine" (ICC-01/22), online at Ukraine | International Criminal Court.

9 Elly Bleier, Human Rights Watch (25 May 2023), online at Fresh Details on Russia's Forcible Transfer of Ukrainian Children | Human Rights Watch.

10 Amy MacKinnon, Foreign Policy (23 February 2024), online at The Ukrainian Children Russia Abducted and Tried to Indoctrinate.

11 Ibid ICC-01/22.

12 Reuters (25 October 2023), online at More than half of Hamas' hostages have foreign nationality—Israel | Reuters. Other open-source reporting puts the total numbers of hostages taken as varying between 220–250 people.

13 Tara Cobham and Tom Watling, *The Independent* (15 February 2025), online at Who are remaining Israeli hostages in Gaza and when might they be freed? | The Independent.

14 C. Anthony Pfaff, "Human Security and the Ethics of Terminating the Conflict in Ukraine," Plenary Presentation to the Joint Professional Military Ethics Working Group (Carlisle, PA: U.S. Army War College, 17 February 2023).

15 Opportunity Cost. BusinessDictionary.com. WebFinance, Inc. http://www.businessdictionary.com/definition/opportunity-cost.html (accessed: April 08, 2018).

16 As a corrective to the organizational effects of moral and spiritual injury (and a general lack of ethical development amongst leaders), I cite with admiration the ten small group recommendations to build a culture of moral courage within the contemporary British Armed Forces. See William Meddings, "Observations of the Conference: Developing Morally Courageous Leaders," in *The Role of Leaders in Building a Culture of Moral Courage: The Proceedings of the Centre for Army Leadership's 2017 Conference* (Sandhurst: Robinson House, 2018), 48–52.

BIBLIOGRAPHY

Ackerman, Elliot. "The Danger Posed by Today's Angry Vets," *The Wall Street Journal,* 10 January 2025, online at The Danger Posed by Today's Angry Vets—WSJ.

American Psychiatric Association. "Definition of Posttraumatic Stress Disorder." In *Diagnostic and Statistical Manual of Mental Disorders (DSM-5),* 1st ed. Washington, DC: American Psychiatric Publishing, 2013.

Alexander, Jonathan. Unpublished Ph.D. Dissertation, *Lethal Autonomous Weapons Systems and the Potential of Moral Injury,* Newport, Rhode Island, Salve Regina University (2024).

Allen, Charles D. and William G. Braun. "Trust: Implications for the Army Profession," in *Military Review* (Sep-Oct 2013): 73–85.

Anderson, Matthew. "Moral Courage: Behind the Magic of Leaders Making the Right Choices" in *The Role of Leaders in Building a Culture of Moral Courage: The Proceedings of the Centre for Army Leadership's 2017 Conference* (Sandhurst, UK: Robinson House, 2018), 37–45.

Antal, Chris J. and Peter D. Yeomans, Rotunda East, Douglas W. Hickey, Solomon Kalkstein, Kimberly M. Brown, and Dana S. Kaminstein. "Transforming Veteran Identity Through Community Engagement: A Chaplain–Psychologist Collaboration to Address Moral Injury," *Journal of Humanistic Psychology* 63/6, SAGE (2023): 801–826.

Augustine, St. *City of God,* ed. Etienne Gibson and trans. Gerald G. Walsh, et. al. New York: Image Books, 1958.

Aquinas, St. Thomas. "Summa Theologiae IIaIIae," in R.W. Dyson, ed., *Aquinas: Political Writings.* Cambridge: University Press, 2002.

Baker, Gerard. "How American Institutions Went from Trust to Bust," *The Wall Street Journal* (8 Sep 2023).

Barnett, Victoria J. "The Ethics of Care for Civilians, Internally Displaced Persons, and Enemy Prisoners of War," in *A Persistent Fire: The Strategic Ethical Impact of World War I on the Global Profession of Arms*, eds. Timothy S. Mallard and Nathan H. White (Washington, DC: National Defense University Press, 2020), 147–163.

Bartow, Omer. "As a former IDF soldier and historian of genocide, I was deeply disturbed by my recent visit to Israel," The Guardian (13 August 2024), online at https://www.theguardian.com/world/article/2024/aug/13/israel-gaza-historian-omer-bartov.

Bayerle, Henry and John Ike, Robert Logan & Ruth Parker. "Sophocles' *Philoctetes* and Moral Injury in the COVID-19 Pandemic," *Journal of Health Communication* 27/2 (2022); 134–139, DOI: https://10.1080/10810730.2022.2054032.

Begby, Endre and Gregory M. Reichberg, and Henrik Syse. "The Ethics of War, Part II: Contemporary Authors and Issues," *Philosophy Compass* 7/5 (2012): 328–347, DOI: https://10.1111/j.1747–9991.2011.00476.x.

Berg, G.E. "The Use of the Computer as a Tool for Assessment and Research in Pastoral Care," in *Journal of Healthcare Chaplaincy* 6/1 (1994): 11–25, DOI https://doi.org/10.1300/J080v06n01_03.

Berdida, Daniel Joseph E. "The Mediating Roles of Moral Courage and Moral Resilience Between Nurses' Moral Distress and Moral Injury: An Online Cross-sectional Study," in *Nurse Education in Practice* 71 (2023): 1013730, DOI: https://10.1016/j.nepr.2023.103730.

Berdida, Daniel Joesph E. and Rizal Angelo N. Grande, "Moral Distress, Moral Resilience, Moral Courage, and Moral Injury Among Nurses in the Philippines During the COVID-19 Pandemic:A Mediation Analysis," in *Journal of Religion and Health* 62 (2023):3957–3978, DOI: https://10.1007/s10943–023–01873-w.

Biggar, Nigel. *In Defence of War.* Oxford, UK: Oxford University Press, 2013.

________. "What Should Christian Ethics Learn from World War I?", in *A Persistent Fire: The Strategic Ethical Impact of World War I on the Global Profession of Arms*, eds. Timothy S. Mallard and Nathan H. White (Washington, DC: National Defense University Press, 2020), 1–20.

Bleier, Elly. *Human Rights Watch* (25 May 2023), online at Fresh Details on Russia's Forcible Transfer of Ukrainian Children | Human Rights Watch.

Bonhoeffer, Dietrich. *Letters and Papers from Prison, DBWE*, Vol. 8. Ed. John W. de Gruchy and trans. Isabel Best, Lisa E. Dahill, Reinhard Kraus, and Nancy Lukens. Minneapolis: Fortress Press, 2009.

________. *Sanctorum Communio: A Theological Study of the Sociology of the Church.* Ed. Clifford Green and trans. Reinhard Krauss and Nancy Lukens. Minneapolis: Fortress Press, 1988.

Borges, Lauren M. and Nazanin H. Bahraini, Brooke Dorsey Holliman, Maura R. Gissen, W. Cole Lawson, and Sean M. Barnes. "Veterans' Perspectives on Discussing Moral Injury in the Context of Evidence-based Psychotherapies for PTSD and Other VA Treatment," in *Journal of Clinical* Psychology 76 (2020):377–391, DOI: https://10.1002/jclp.22887.

Brock, Rita Nakashima and Gabriella Lettini. *Soul Repair: Recovering from Moral Injury After War.* Boston: Beacon Press, 2012.

Brodrick, William. *The Discourtesy of Death.* New York: The Overlook Press, 2013.

Bryan, Craig J. and AnnaBelle O. Bryan, Michael D. Anestis, Joye C. Anestis, Bradley A. Green, Neysa Etienne, Chad E. Morrow, and Bobbie Ray-Sannerud. "Measuring Moral Injury: Psychometric Properties of the Moral Injury Events Scale in Two Military Samples," in *Assessment* 23/5 (2016): 557–570, DOI: https://10.1177/1073191115590855.

Business Dictionary.com, "Opportunity Cost", *WebFinance, Inc.* (8 April 2018), online at http://www.businessdictionary.com/definition/opportunity-cost.html.

Cahill, Jonathan M. and Ashley J. Moyse, and Lydia S. Dugdale. "Ruptured Selves: Moral Injury and Wounded Identity," in *Medicine, Health Care and Philosophy* 26 (2023): 225–231, DOI: https://10.1007/s11019–023–10138-y.

Carey, Lindsay et. al. "Moral Injury, Spiritual Care and the Role of Chaplains: An Exploratory Scoping Review of Literature and Resources," in *Journal of Religion and Health* 55/14 (August 2016): 1218–1245.

Clark, Allen. *Wounded Soldier, Healing Warrior.* St. Paul, MN: Zenith, 2007.

von Clausewitz, Carl. *On War.* Ithaca, NY: Cornell University Press, 1973.

Cleland, Max. *Strong at the Broken Places.* Waco, TX: Word Books, 1980.

Cobham, Tara and Tom Watling. *The Independent* (15 February 2025), online at Who are remaining Israeli hostages in Gaza and when might they be freed? | The Independent.

Cook, Martin L. "Ethical Issues in War: An Overview," in *The U.S. Army War College Guide to National Security Issues, Vol. II: National Security Policy and Strategy*, ed. J. Boone Bartholomees. Carlisle, PA: Strategic Studies Institute, 2012: 217–227.

_______. *The Moral Warrior: Ethics and Service in the U.S. Military.* Albany, NY: SUNY Press, 2004.

Currier, Joseph M. and Jason M. Holland, Kent Drescher and David Foy, "Initial Psychometric Evaluation of the Moral Injury Questionnaire—Military Version," in *Clinical Psychology and Psychotherapy* 22 (2015): 54–63, DOI: https://10.1002/cpp.1866.

Dallaire, Roméo. *Shake Hands with the Devil: The Failure of Humanity in Rwanda.* London: Arrow Books, 2004.

Danto, Arthur C. "On Moral Codes and Modern War." In *War, Morality, and the Modern Military Profession*, Ed. Malham M. Wakin (Boulder, CO: Westview Press, 1979); 473–486.

Department of the Army, ADP 3–0, *Operations.* Washington, DC: HQ, Department of the Army, 31 July 2019.

_______. FM 16–1, *Religious Support.* Washington, DC: HQ, Department of the Army, 21 January 2019.

Department of Defense, JP 3–0, *Joint Campaigns and Operations.* Washington, DC: The Joint Staff, 18 June 2022.

Dewey, Larry. *War and Redemption: Treatment and Recovery in Combat-related Posttraumatic Stress Disorder.* Burlington, VT: Ashgate Publishing Co., 2004.

Dubik, James M. *Just War Reconsidered: Strategy, Ethics, and Theory.* Lexington, KY: University Press of Kentucky Press, 2016.

Eikenaar, Teun, "Relating to Moral Injuries: Dutch Mental Health Practitioners on Moral Injury Among Military and Police Workers," in *Social Science and Medicine* 298 (2022): 114876, DOI: https://10.1016/j.socscimed.2022.114876.

Elshtain, Jean Bethke. *Sovereignty: God, State, and Self.* New York: Basic Books, 2008.

Edwards, Simon. *Soldier of Hope: Lessons from the International Community in Recovery and Growth from Battlefield Trauma and Mental Health.* London: The Winston Churchill Memorial Trust, 2016.

Farr, Thomas. "Theology and International Religious Liberty," Plenary Remarks to the Christianity and National Security Conference 2017, Washington, DC, online at Thomas Farr Christianity & National Security 2017: Theology & International Religious Liberty—Providence.

Fleming, Wesley H. "Complex Moral Injury: Shattered Moral Assumptions," *Journal of Religion and Health* 61 (2022): 1022–1050, DOI: https://10.1007/s10943–022–01542–4.

Friedman, Leon, ed. *The Law of War: A Documentary History—Vol. II.* New York: Random House, 1972.

1. "Court-Martial of William L. Calley, Jr. (1971)"—pgs. 1703–1728. Transcript focuses on LT Calley's understanding of his company commander's intent (CPT Medina) to permit unrestricted targeting of civilians in My Lai hamlet in order to eradicate Viet Cong and North Vietnamese Army forces interspersed in the populace.
2. "Court-Martial of Ernest L. Medina (1971)"–pgs. 1729–1738. Transcript focuses on CPT Medina's understanding of his commander's intent (provided to LT Calley) to use appropriate Rules of Engagement in order to search and destroy enemy combatants in and around the My Lai hamlet.

Fuson, J. E. "A Pastoral Counselling Model for Leading Post-Combat Christian Soldiers Experiencing Spiritual Injury to Spiritual Health Through Examining the Biblical Concepts of Evil,

Pain, Abandonment, and Forgiveness." Biola University (2013) ProQuest Dissertation and Theses, 1303015706.

Graham, Larry Kent. *Moral Injury: Restoring Wounded Souls.* Nashville: Abingdon Press, 2017.

Harman, Jane and Eric Eidelman, et al., *Report of the Commission on the National Defense Strategy.* Washington, DC: The Rand Organization, 29 July 2024, online at Commission on the National Defense Strategy | RAND.

Hartle, Anthony E. *Moral Issues in Military Decision Making*, 2nd ed. Lawrence, KA: University of Kansas Press, 2004.

Hemingway, Ernest. "In Another Country," in *Women, Men and the Great War: An Anthology of Stories*, ed. Trudi Tate (Manchester: Manchester University Press, 1995): 121–124.

________. "Soldier's Home," in *The Complete Short Stories of Ernest Hemingway: The Finca Gigía Edition* (New York: Charles Scribner's Sons,1987): 111–116.

International Centre for Moral Injury. "What Is Moral Injury? (27 November 2024), online at What is Moral Injury?—Durham University.

International Criminal Court. "Situation in Ukraine" (ICC–01/22), online at Ukraine | International Criminal Court.

Jones, Edgar, Nicola Fear and Simon Wessely. "Shell Shock and Mild Traumatic Brain Injury: A Historical Review," in *American Journal of Psychiatry*, 164/11 (2007): 1641–1645.

Jones, Jeffrey M., "Confidence in U.S. Institutions Down; Average at New Low," *Gallup* (5 July 2022) online at Confidence in U.S. Institutions Down; Average at New Low.

Johnson, James D. *Combat Chaplain: A Thirty-year Vietnam Battle.* Denton, TX: Univeristy of North Texas Press, 2001.

Johnson, James T. *Morality and Contemporary Warfare.* New Haven: Yale University Press, 2001.

Johnson, Rear Adm. Joyce, D.O. "Moral Injury," *Military Officer* (July 2017): 48.

Junger, Sebastian. "How PTSD Became a Problem Far Beyond the Battlefield." *Vanity Fair Magazine* (June 2015).

Kelle, Brad E. *Moral Injury: A Guidebook for Understanding and Engagement* (London: Lexington Books, 2020).

________. *The Bible and Moral Injury: Reading Scripture Alongside War's Unseen Wounds.* Nashville: Abingdon Press, 2020.

Khettache, Assala, "The Weaponization of Collective Moral Injuries in Africa," the 2024 Robbins Lecture, the International Centre for Moral Injury, Durham, UK.

Klay, Phil. *Redeployment.* New York: Penguin Press, 2014.

Koenig, Harold G. and Tyler J. VanderWeele and John R. Peteet, "Understanding the Religion- Physical Health Relationship," in *Handbook of Religion and Health*, 3rd ed. Oxford: Oxford University Press, , 2024.

Layson, Mark and Lindsay Carey. "Moral Injury Narratives and the Role of Chaplains in the Australian Context: A Bio-Psycho-Social-Spiritual Approach to Prevention and Treatment," Paper Presentation at the International Centre for Moral Injury Annual Conference, Durham, UK, 22–24 April 2024.

Lechner, John. *Death is Our Business: Russian Mercenaries and the New Era of Private Warfare.* New York: Bloomsbury Publishing, 2025.

Lee, Mark C. "Growth After Trauma: Moral Injury, PTSD, and PTG." In *A Persistent Fire: The Strategic Ethical Impact of World War I on the Global Profession of Arms*, eds. Timothy S. Mallard and Nathan H. White (Washington, DC: National Defense University Press, 2020): 247–272.

Lewis, Adrian. "Conscription, the Republic, and America's Future," *Military Review* (November-December 2009): 15–24.

Lewis, C. S. *Till We Have Faces: A Myth Retold.* New York: Harper Collins, 2012.

Litz, Brett T. and Leslie Lebowitz, Matt J. Gray, and William P. Nash. *Adaptive Disclosure: A New Treatment for Military Trauma, Loss, and Moral Injury.* New York: The Guilford Press, 2016.

LiVecche, Marc. *The Good Kill: Just War and Moral Injury.* Oxford, UK: Oxford University Press, 2021.

________. "Military Necessity as Imperative: Just War and Hiroshima," in *Military Necessity and Just War Statecraft: The Principle of National Security Stewardship*, eds. Eric Patterson and Marc LiVecche. London: Routledge, 2023.

________."The Fifth Image: Seeing the Enemy With Just War Eyes," in *PROVIDENCE* (Summer 2016): 50–56.

Lucas, Jr., George R. "This Is Not Your Father's War'—Confronting the Moral Challenges of 'Unconventional' War," *Journal of National Security Law & Policy* 3/329 (2009): 329–340.

Lykke, Jr., Arthur F. "Defining Military Strategy," *Military Review* (January-February 1997): 183–186.

McDonald, Joseph, "What is Moral Injury?", in *Moral Injury: A Guidebook for Understanding and Engagement*, ed. Brad E. Kelle (Lantham, MD: Lexington Books, 2020): 7–20.

MacKinnon, Amy. *Foreign Policy* (23 February 2024), online at The Ukrainian Children Russia Abducted and Tried to Indoctrinate.

MacIntosh, Duncan. "Posttraumatic Stress Disorder Weaponized: A Theory of Moral Injury?" in Justin T. McDaniel (ed.), *Preventing and Treating the Invisible Wounds of War: Combat Trauma, Moral Injury, and Psychological Health* (Oxford: Oxford University Press, 2023): 175–206.

Maguen, Shira and Bret Litz. "Moral Injury in Veterans of War," *Research Quarterly* 23/1 (2012): 1–6.

_______. "Moral Injury in the Context of War," U.S. Department of Veterans Affairs National Center for PTSD, online at http://www.ptsd.va.gov/professional/co-occurring/moral_injury_at_war.asp.

Marlantes, Karl. *What It Is Like to Go to War*. New York: Atlantic Monthly Press, 2011.

Mallard, Timothy. Unpublished Ph.D. Dissertation, *Marginality as Power: The Ecclesiology of Dietrich Bonhoeffer as a Construct for Public Theology Through the United States Army Chaplain Corps*, Lampeter, Wales; University of Wales Trinity Saint David (2015).

_______."Twin Children of the Great War: Assessing the Effects of Moral and Spiritual Injury Today." In *A Persistent Fire: The Strategic Ethical Impact of World War I on the Global Profession of Arms*, eds. Timothy S. Mallard and Nathan H. White (Washington, DC: National Defense University Press, 2020): 273–295.

Mansfield, Stephen. *The Faith of the American Soldier.* New York: Tarcher Press, 2005.

Marshall, George C. *The Papers of George Catlett Marshall,* ed. Larry I. Bland, Sharon Ritenour Stevens, and Clarence E. Wunderlin, Jr. (Lexington, VA: The George C. Marshall Foundation, 1981–). Electronic version based on *The Papers of George Catlett Marshall,* vol. 2, *"We Cannot Delay," July 1, 1939-December 6, 1941* (Baltimore and London: The Johns Hopkins University Press, 1986); pp. 534–538.

Mattox, John Mark. "The Moral Foundations of Army Officership," in *the Future of the Army Profession*, 2nd Ed., ed. Lloyd J. Matthews (New York: McGraw-Hill Publishing, 2005): 387–408.

Meagher, Robert E. and Douglas A. Pryer. *War and Moral Injury: A Reader* (Eugene, OR: Wipf & Stock Publishers, 2018).

Meddings, William. "Observations of the Conference: Developing Morally Courageous Leaders," in *The Role of Leaders in Building a Culture of Moral Courage: The Proceedings of the Centre for Army Leadership's 2017 Conference* (Sandhurst, UK: Robinson House, 2018): 48–52.

"Ten Observations:

1. We must develop leaders who accept individual moral responsibility.

2. We must consider if greater risk aversion and fear of being held accountable for actions will inhibit the growth of junior leaders.

3. We must develop leaders to encourage a "Growth Mind-set" to encourage responsible leadership.

4. We must develop leaders with the humility to admit they can still improve as leaders.

5. We must develop leaders who scrutinize positive feedback much more intensely that they do negative feedback (360 feedback may be one mechanism to assist this).

6. Our leader development programmes must exercise moral courage and morality in the same way they exercise command and tactical judgment.

7. To develop moral courage we must use enforcement and sanctions that create consequences for immorality.

8. Leaders must build a link between their follower's values, the organisation's values and the emotions the organisation create (sic).

9. As well as helping followers understand the organisation's values, leaders must make exercising moral courage less risky to followers.

10. Leaders must encourage debate, discussion and healthy conflict."

Meredith, Lisa S., et. al. *Promoting Psychological Resilience in the U.S. Military.* (Washington, DC: Rand Center for Military and Health Policy Research, 2011..

McGill, Arthur. *Suffering: A Test of Theological Method.* Philadelphia: Westminster Press, 1982.

Niebuhr, Reinhold. *The Nature and Destiny of Man, Vol 1: Human Nature: A Christian Interpretation* and *Vol 2: Human Destiny: A Christian Interpretation.* New York: Charles Scribner's Sons, 1964.

Nye, Joseph. "Is This the End of Soft Power?" *Financial Times* (8–9 March 2025): FT Weekend 1–2.

________. *Understanding International Conflicts: An Introduction to Theory and History.* New York: Longman, 2003.

Office of the Director of National Intelligence, *Annual Threat Assessment of the U.S. Intelligence Community* (Washington, DC: ODNI, 5 February 2024), available at ATA-2024-Unclassified-Report.pdf.

Ogletree, Thomas W. "Agents and Moral Formation," in *The Blackwell Companion to Religious Ethics*, ed. William Schweiker (Oxford: Blackwell Publishing, 2005): 36–44.

Orend, Brian. *The Morality of War.* Peterborough, ONT: Broadview Press, 2006.

Owens, Macubin. "Force Planning: The Crossroads of Strategy and the Political Process," *Orbis* 59/3 (2015): 411–437.

Patterson, Eric. "Christian Realism, Christian Nationalism(s), and Religious Freedom," *Providence* (12 December 2024), online at Christian Realism, Nationalism(s), and Religious Freedom—Providence.

_______. "Eight Principles for Christian Realism," Providence (23 September 2020), online at Eight Principles for Christian Realism—Providence.

Percy, Jennifer. "The Priest of Abu Ghraib," *The Smithsonian* 49/9 (January-February 2019): 44–55.

Petit, Philip. "Consequentialism," in *A Companion to Ethics*, Peter Singer (ed.) (Oxford: Blackwell Publishing, 1993): 231–240.

Pfaff, C. Anthony. "Human Security and the Ethics of Terminating the Conflict in Ukraine," Plenary Presentation to the Joint Professional Military Ethics Working Group. Carlisle, PA: U.S. Army War College, 17 February 2023.

Powers, Brian. "Christian Theology and Moral Injury," in *Moral Injury: A Guidebook for Understanding and Engagement*, ed. Brad Kelle (London: Roman & Littlefield, 2020): 189–200.

_______. *Full Darkness: Original Sin, Moral Injury, and Wartime Violence.* Grand Rapids, MI: William. B. Eerdmans, 2019.

Ramsay, Nancy and Carrie Doehring, eds., *Military Moral Injury and Spiritual Care.* Saint Louis, MO: Chalice Press, 2019.

Reuters (4 April 2022), online at Russia says footage in Ukraine's Bucha was 'ordered' to blame Russia | Reuters.

_______. (25 October 2023), online at More than half of Hamas' hostages have foreign nationality—Israel | Reuters.

Rittel, Horst W. J. and Melvin M. Weber, "Planning Problems Are Wicked Problem," in *Developments in Design Methodology*, ed. Nigel Cross (Chichester, NY: John Wiley & Sons, 1984); 135–144.

Romesha, Clinton. *Red Platoon.* New York: Dutton, 2016.

Sacks, Jonathan. *Morality: Restoring the Common Good in Trying Times.* New York: Basic Books, 2020.

Sassoon, Siegfried. *Memoirs of An Infantry Officer.* London: Faber & Faber, 1930.

Shay, Jonathan. *Achilles in Vietnam: Combat Trauma and the Undoing of Character.* New York: Scribner, 2003.

_______. "Moral Injury," *Psychoanalytic Psychology* 31/2 (2014): 182–191.

_______. *Odyssesus in America: Combat Trauma and the Trials of Homecoming.* New York: Scribner, 2002.

Sherman, Nancy. *Afterwar: Healing the Moral Wounds of Our Soldiers.* Oxford, UK: Oxford University Press, 2015.

Smith, Michael. "Realism," in *A Companion to Ethics*, Peter Singer, ed. (Oxford: Blackwell Publishing, 1993): 399–410.

Solzhenitsyn, Alexander. "The Exhausted West," *Harvard Magazine* 80/6 (July-August 1978).

Sophocles, *Oedipus the King and Other Tragedies: Oedipus the King, Aias, Philoctetes, Oedipus at Colonus.* Oxford, UK: Oxford University Press, 2015.

Snider, Don M. "The U.S. Army as Profession," in *The Future of the Army Profession*, 2nd ed., ed. Lloyd J. Matthews (New York: McGraw-Hill, 2005): 1–17.

_______. "Will Army 2025 be a Military Profession?" in *Parameters* 45/4 (2015): 39–51, online at https://doi/10.55540/0031–1723.2985.

Strasser, Steven, ed. *The Abu Ghraib Investigations: The Official Reports of the Independent Panel and the Pentagon on the Shocking Prisoner Abuse in Iraq.* New York: Public Affairs, 2004.

Sweeney, Patrick J. and Louis W. Fry, "Character Development Through Spiritual Leadership," in *Consulting Psychology Journal: Practice and Research* 64/2 (2012): 89–107.

Sweeney, Patrick J. and Jeffrey E. Rhodes and Bruce Boling, "Spiritual Fitness: A Key Component of Total Force Fitness," *Joint Force Quarterly* 66 (3rd Quarter 2012): 35–41.

Szandzik, Eric James. "President Clinton's Nonintervention in the Rwanda Genocide: An Analysis of U.S. Presidential Foreign Policy Decisions," in *World Affairs* 185/1 (2022): 176–206, online at https://doi.org/10.1177/00438200211064941.

Tick, Edward. *War and the Soul: Healing Our Nation's Veterans from Posttraumatic Stress Disorder.* Wheaton, IL: Quest Publishing, 2005.

Thielicke, Helmut. *How to Believe Again.* Minneapolis: Fortress Press, 1972.

Thornton, Martin. *English Spirituality: An Outline of Ascetical Theology According to the English Pastoral Tradition.* Cambridge, MA: Cowley Publications, 1986.

Tomlin, Graham. *The Prodigal Spirit: The Trinity, the Church and the Future of the World.* London: Alpha International, 2011.

Tournier, Paul. *The Whole Person in a Broken World.* Transl. John and Helen Doberstein. New York: Harper & Row, 1964.

U.S. Army Combined Arms Center, FM 7–22, C1, *Holistic Health and* Fitness. Washington, DC: HQ Department of the Army, 8 October 2020.

U.S. Army Peacekeeping and Stability Operations Institute, *Mass Atrocity Prevention and Response Options: A Policy Planning Handbook.* Carlisle, PA: PKSOI, 2012, online at MAPRO_handbook_final.pdf.

U.N. Office of the High Commissioner for Human Rights. Press Release (7 December 2022), online at UN report details summary executions of civilians by Russian troops in northern Ukraine | OHCHR.

U.S. Commission on International Religious Freedom, *2024 Annual Report*, online at Annual Reports | USCIRF.

U.S. Department of Veterans Affairs, *2023 National Veteran Suicide Prevention Annual Report.* Washington, DC: Office of Mental Health and Suicide Prevention, 1 November 2023.

U.S. Navy Culture and Force Resilience Office, *Warrior Toughness Readiness Guide*, in the *Forged by the Sea Culture of Readiness Program 2.0.* Washington, DC: USNAVCFRO,# March 2024.

Vanden Brook, Tom, "Senior Military Officials Sanctioned for More Than 500 Cases of Serious Misconduct," *USA Today* (24 October 2017), online at https://www.usatoday.com/story/news/politics/2017/10/24/generals-sex-misconduct- pentagon-army-sanctions-hagel-gillibrand/794770001/.

VanderWeele, TJ, Wortham JS, Carey LB, Case BW, Cowden RG, Duffee C, Jackson-Meyer K, Lu F, Mattson SA, Padgett RN, Peteet JR, Rutledge J, Symons X and Koenig HG (2025) "Moral Trauma, Moral Distress, Moral Injury, and Moral Injury Disorder: Definitions and Assessments," *Front. Psychol.* 16:1422441. DOI: https://10.3389/fpsyg.2025.1422441.

Volf, Miroslav. *A Public Faith: How Followers of Christ Should Serve the Common Good.* Grand Rapids: Brazos Press, 2011.

Walzer, Michael. *Arguing About War.* New Haven, CT: Yale University Press, 2005.

_______.*Just and Unjust Wars: A Moral Argument with Historical Illustrations— 4th ed.* New York: Basic Books, 2006.

Wernau, Julie, "U.S. Suicides Reached a Record High Last Year," *The Wall Street Journal* (29 November 2023).

Wheeler, Nathan. "For a Holy Priesthood: A Petrine Model for Evangelical Cultural Engagement," *Journal of the Evangelical Theological Society* 59/3 (September 2016): 523–539.

White, Nathan H. "Toward a Resilient Military Ethic," in *A Persistent Fire: The Strategic Ethical Impact of World War I on the Global Profession of Arms,* eds. Timothy S. Mallard and Nathan H. White (Washington, DC: National Defense University Press, 2020): 337–352.

Wood, David. *What Have We Done: The Moral Injury of Our Longest Wars.* New York: Little, Brown and Company, 2016.

Wong, Leonard and Steven J. Gerras. *Veteran Disability Compensation and the Army Profession: Good Intentions Gone Awry.* Carlisle, PA: U.S. Army War College Press, 29 Jan 2021, online at Veteran Disability Compensation and the Army Profession: Good Intentions Gone Awry.

Weigel, George. *The Cube and the Cathedral: Europe, America, and Politics Without God.* Leominster, UK: Gracewing, 2005.

_______. *Tranquillitas Ordinis: The Present Failure and Future Promise of American Catholic Thought on War and Peace.* New York: Oxford University Press, 1987.

INDEX

F

G

H

I

J

L

M

S

T

U

V

W

ABOUT THE AUTHOR

Timothy Mallard, is a Professor of Leadership and Ethics at Birmingham Theological Seminary and a Visiting Research Fellow at St. Chad's College and Durham University (UK). He recently retired from almost 37 years as a U.S. Army chaplain and holds a Ph.D. in Theological Ethics from the University of Wales Trinity Saint David and an M.S.S. in Strategic Leadership from the U.S. Army War College. In his military career, he deployed as a Battalion, Brigade, and Division Chaplain to combat operations in Saudi Arabia, Kuwait, Afghanistan, and Iraq and held strategic postings at both US Army Europe-Africa and the Pentagon. His official military decorations include two awards each of the Legion of Merit and Bronze Star medals, the Combat Action Badge and the Purple Heart.